The Inner World in the Outer World

◼ The Inner World in the Outer World

Psychoanalytic Perspectives

Edited by Edward R. Shapiro, M.D.

Yale University Press/New Haven & London

Designed by Nancy Ovedovitz and set in Janson Text type by The Composing Room of Michigan, Inc. Printed in the United States of America by Vail-Ballou Press, Binghamton, New York.

Library of Congress Cataloging-in-Publication Data

The inner world in the outer world : psychoanalytic perspectives / edited by Edward R. Shapiro.
    p.   cm.
Includes bibliographical references and index.
ISBN 0-300-06528-0 (cloth : alk. paper)
1. Psychoanalysis. 2. Self-presentation. 3. Schemas (Psychology).
I. Shapiro, Edward R., 1941–   .
BF175.I555 1997
150.19'5—dc20   96-8261
                                                             CIP

A catalogue record for this book is available from the British Library.

The paper in this book meets the guidelines for permanence and durability of the Committee on Production Guidelines for Book Longevity of the Council on Library Resources.

10 9 8 7 6 5 4 3 2 1

For the staff and patients at the Austen Riggs Center.

You hold an important place for examined living in an increasingly unexamined and chaotic world.

Contents

Acknowledgments   ix

List of Contributors   xi

Introduction   1
      Edward R. Shapiro, M.D.

1 The Boundaries Are Shifting: Renegotiating
the Therapeutic Frame   7
      Edward R. Shapiro, M.D.

2 Conformity and Individualism   27
      Roy Schafer, Ph.D.

3 The Private Self and Relational Theory   43
        Arnold H. Modell, M.D.

4 On the Relationship of Dream Content, Trauma,
and Mind: A View from Inside Out or Outside In?   59
        C. Brooks Brenneis, Ph.D.

5 The Artist and the Outer World   77
        Joyce McDougall, D.Ed.

6 Ideology and Bureaucracy as Social Defenses
Against Aggression   97
        Otto F. Kernberg, M.D.

7 On Discourse with an Enemy   123
        H. Shmuel Erlich, Ph.D.

8 Remembering Iphigenia: Voice, Resonance,
and the Talking Cure   143
        Carol Gilligan, Ph.D.

9 Psychoanalytic Institutions in a Changing World   169
        Anton Obholzer, M.D.

Index   183

Acknowledgments

This book emerged from an international conference held at the Austen Riggs Center to celebrate its seventy-fifth anniversary. A staggering amount of work was necessary to bring more than three hundred people from nine countries and twenty-eight states to Stockbridge, Massachusetts, to hear this distinguished group of presenters. I am very grateful to Riggs' senior staff. Drs. James Sacksteder, John Muller, and M. Gerard Fromm helped develop the conference, choose the speakers, review the papers, and manage the academic event. Dr. Eric Plakun helped me to think about the relation of external limitations to internal conflict. Julie Martino, administrative secretary to four medical directors, organized the anniversary celebration and welcomed everyone, pulling together the missing pieces. The Rapaport-Klein Study Group at Riggs authorized a joint Scientific Prize for former staff and fellows of Riggs, attracting the papers of C. Brooks Brenneis and Shmuel Erlich. Dr. Ess White organized an extraordinary alumni reunion—for former patients and staff—providing a vital context for this thinking.

In the hectic world of health care, directing a hospital does not easily allow for writing time. My wife, Dr. Donna Elmendorf, joined me in this task, shared the anxiety, helped me to think clearly, and provided time and space for me to work.

Contributors

C. Brooks Brenneis, Ph.D., clinical associate professor, department of psychiatry, and lecturer, department of psychology, University of Wisconsin—Madison.

H. Shmuel Erlich, Ph.D., Sigmund Freud Professor of Psychoanalysis and director, Sigmund Freud Center for Study and Research in Psychoanalysis, Hebrew University of Jerusalem; training and supervising analyst, Israel Psychoanalytic Society and Institute.

Carol Gilligan, Ph.D., professor of education, Harvard University.

Otto F. Kernberg, M.D., professor of psychiatry, Cornell University Medical College; training and supervising analyst, Columbia University Center for Psychoanalytic Training and

Research; associate chairman and medical director, New York Hospital-Cornell Medical Center, Westchester Division.

Joyce McDougall, D.Ed., training and supervising analyst, Paris Psychoanalytic Institute and Society.

Arnold H. Modell, M.D., clinical professor of psychiatry, Harvard Medical School; training and supervising analyst, Boston Psychoanalytic Institute.

Anton Obholzer, M.D., B.Sc., M.B., Ch.B., D.P.M., FRC Psych., consultant psychiatrist and chief executive, Tavistock and Portman Clinic Trust, London.

Roy Schafer, Ph.D., training and supervising analyst, Columbia University Center for Psychoanalytic Training and Research.

Edward R. Shapiro, M.D., medical director and chief executive officer, Austen Riggs Center; director, Erik H. Erikson Institute for Education and Research at Riggs; associate clinical professor of psychiatry, Harvard Medical School; faculty, Boston Psychoanalytic Institute.

The Inner World in the Outer World

Edward R. Shapiro, M.D.

■ Introduction

Rapid social change is overwhelming the individual. The increasing noise of the media, the frantic pace of international competition, and the pressures of massive economic interdependency are robbing us of emotional space for internal reflection. Even the previously accepted settings for internal reflection—the ritual of religion, the stability of family structure, the discipline of rigorous education—are in disarray. The cacaphony of stimulation and the lack of familiar structures interfere with time to focus on and develop our internal worlds. In psychiatry, attention to patients' internal lives is disappearing, as emphasis is given to management of external symptoms through biological and behavioral interventions. Psychiatric diagnosis is no longer a dynamic formulation of internal conflict and tension, but a categorization of external behaviors and symptoms. In the health care system, fiscal crisis is leading to efforts to control costs through managed-care proposals for quick solutions to complex problems. Clinical staff no longer have time to attend to patients' fantasies and conflicts. The number of persons in full-time psychoanalytic practice is diminishing. Outer-world changes are pressuring us all.

While many dynamically oriented thinkers bemoan the end of a golden era of analytic reflection, others find an opportunity for creative thinking. After all, any attempt to separate the inner from the outer world is artificial; the two are in dynamic interaction. We make meaning out of our experiences, and experience itself is at the boundary between the two worlds—external interaction and internal interpretation. Psychoanalysis focuses on the individual's created world. But as we have deepened the theory and attended to the analytic situation, we have increasingly noticed the influence of the other—the analyst, the family, the larger social network—on that internal creation. We no longer believe that the analyst is simply a neutral interpreter of the experiencing patient.

A century ago, at the beginning of psychoanalysis, the theory did not attend to the analyst's personality. This silent, tactical decision was essential to reduce the complexity of the data and focus on the patient's inner workings. More recently, psychoanalytic theory has moved to study the analyst's contribution to the dyad. This has opened the possibility of integrating the interpersonal, the contextual. The notion of the "bipersonal field" (Langs, 1976) is now part of mainstream psychoanalytic thought. In the past several decades, with early childhood studies on the role of the father (Abelin, 1971), Lacan's focus on the symbolic contribution of culture (Lacan, 1975), Ogden's formulation of "analyst-patient intersubjectivity" (Ogden, 1994), and the re-examination of Erik Erikson's ideas after his death in 1994, the larger context is making itself felt in psychoanalytic theory.

Speculative studies that go beyond the consulting room have always pushed the theory painstakingly developed from the clinical encounter. These speculations lead the field. In this book, a group of analytic thinkers explore the boundary between the inner and outer worlds from wide-ranging perspectives. They raise provocative questions. These authors gathered at an international symposium to celebrate the seventy-fifth anniversary of the Austen Riggs Center in Stockbridge, Massachusetts. They found this topic a useful focus for celebrating the ongoing commitment at Austen Riggs to the intensive psychodynamic study of the individual in context. In the maelstrom of social change, the Austen Riggs Center has found a way to join the outer world while holding a focused attention on the inner world.

The book opens with Edward R. Shapiro's suggestion that dynamic therapists' limited focus on the internal world may have contributed to the field's inability to stay in touch with the effects of massive social change on the treatment setting. In the contemporary world, there is less time available for sustained intimacy. This places the extended intimacy of the analytic dyad under unexaminable social pressure through projection and envy. In such a social context, therapists can lose perspective, developing defenses of delusional intimacy or defensive hyper-management. Shapiro suggests that attention to the limits of external resources and the dynamic meaning of those limits focuses the framework of treatment, facilitating an increased capacity to sustain an interpretive stance.

Roy Schafer looks at patients with the social behaviors of conformity and individualism, asking how such diverse external adaptations can reveal striking internal similarities. These individuals focus their attention outward in rigidly controlled presentations, reflecting their flight from the chaotic stimulation of their internal lives. Schafer describes these patients' dread of the ambiguity inherent in an evolving identity, or an "identity at risk." He then expands his discussion to explore conformity and individualism as they appear in the role identifications and countertransferences of therapists.

Arnold H. Modell orients us toward psychoanalytic theory, describing the paradox of a self that is both private and social. He notes, "The self obtains its sense of continuity from within yet at the same time is dependent upon the appraisal of others who can either support or disrupt the self's continuity" and adds, "In closing oneself off from others, one inadvertently closes oneself off from oneself." Modell is exploring the boundary between private and social from the perspective of dependency and autonomy: how can one maintain one's own voice in the midst of the other person?

C. Brooks Brenneis takes on the controversy about the role of external trauma in the development of the mind. Is there an internal life that adapts the most traumatic external experience into a shape determined by the individual's character? Or is external trauma so powerful that it can bypass our meaning generators and appear directly in our dreams? Brenneis carefully reviews the clinical and experimental literature, revealing the texture of the emotionally formed metaphors and structural processes that articulate the boundary between internal and external worlds.

Joyce McDougall examines this boundary as represented by creative art. She argues that creativity derives from the erogenic body and its functions, structured by the caretakers of infancy. The creative work, like Winnicott's transitional object, is neither inside nor outside; the medium is an aspect of the creator's self. The public, too, is originally an internal object, placed in the outer world. The artist can experience outer-world stimulation as pregenital sexuality, and his or her creative efforts as retaliative damage to or repair of the outside. McDougall offers several case studies which illuminate the interpenetration of the inner-outer world boundary through the creative act.

Moving further into the social world, Otto F. Kernberg describes the social structuring of aggression. He argues that aggression, ordinarily under control in the relatively restricted dyadic and triadic relationships of individuals, couples, and families, can be expressed vicariously through group and organizational processes. Kernberg suggests that the large group—read "society"—protects itself from impending aggression by processes of ad hoc ideology formation and bureaucratization. These defenses can contribute to two outcomes: dependent and narcissistic group behavior that is satisfied by a reassuring mediocrity in the leader, or paranoid mobs that support violent revolutionary ideology and totalitarian leadership. He describes how reduction in resources and incompetence in leaders contribute to paranoia in social organizations, and he elaborates how ideology and bureaucratization evolve as defensive structures.

H. Shmuel Erlich explores the internal and group forces that interfere with our ability to have discourse with those we perceive as "the enemy." The "enemy" is an outer-world notion, yet the experience of enmity is riddled with internal pressures; it is one of the most dangerous conjunctions of the inner and outer world. Like the creative acts McDougall describes, enmity is at the boundary between internal and external reality, between self and otherness, between individual and group phenomena. Erlich distinguishes preoedipal from oedipal enemies, suggesting that we can dare talk only with the latter. He affirms the need for a "third," mediated by symbols, which allows a dangerous dyad to notice their common ground.

Carol Gilligan brings us to child development and the impact of the social world on voice and resonance. She asks, "How does the learning derived from female development offer a possible integration of a culturally sanctioned, patriarchal dissociation between the inner and outer worlds?" Through the study of Agamemnon's martyred daughter Iphigenia, Gilligan reviews the pressures of the outer world on the differing development of boys and girls. The boy separates the inner and outer worlds in early childhood to join his father; the girl holds onto the boundary until adolescence. This developmental difference suggests a deeper meaning of connection—not only to another, but between the inner and outer worlds. In adolescence, the girl's distinct voice can disappear. What is required is a relationship mediated by words and a resonant responsiveness that may be obscured by a patriarchal culture.

Finally, Anton Obholzer looks at the changes that psychoanalytically oriented institutions must make if their missions are to survive in a rapidly changing world. He notes that we have shifted in our experience of the world from the "us versus them" split that characterized East-West relations to a more internal "domestic" focus on the economics of social organizations: health care, business, education, and law and order. We have become disillusioned with the dynamics of dependency. As a consequence, the role of the "all-knowing" professional is under attack in society. To grapple with these changes and join the world more fully, psychoanalytic institutions can shift their focus from professional insularity toward broader applications, from "pure" research to outcome research, from professionalism to consumerism, and from consultation to management. He argues that our value as a discipline lies in our capacity for the integrated approach reflected in the title of this book: to attend to the individual *within* the social context.

These chapters introduce the reader to the boundary between the inner world and the outer world. The first and last chapters are written by the leaders of two psychoanalytic institutions—the Austen Riggs Center and the Tavistock Clinic, respectively. They represent institutional engagement with that world that presses heavily on the individual's internal space. The struggles of psychoanalytic institutions to survive with their missions intact help to provide the social space within which—as all nine authors illustrate—we can further elaborate the texture of the boundary between the inner and outer worlds. It is on this boundary that we live.

REFERENCES

Abelin, E. L. (1971). The role of the father in separation-individuation. In *Separation-Individuation: Essays in Honor of Margaret Mahler,* ed. J. McDevitt and C. Settlage. New York: International Universities Press, pp. 229–252.

Lacan, J. (1975). *The Seminar: Book I.* Cambridge: Cambridge University Press. 1988.

Langs, R. (1976). *The Bipersonal Field.* New York: Aronson.

Ogden, T. H. (1994). The analytical third: Working with intersubjective clinical facts. *International Journal of Psycho-analysis,* 75:3–20.

Edward R. Shapiro, M.D.

■ 1 The Boundaries Are Shifting: Renegotiating the Therapeutic Frame

Psychodynamic treatment is under siege. Shifting societal values and increasing economic pressures are shaking the structures of our work. In this chapter, I shall examine this crisis by looking at the phenomenology and current treatment of personality disorders. Using this illness as a lens, I shall examine the impact of current pressures on therapists' ability to establish a reliable framework for dynamic treatment. Such a framework has always included the interplay of interpretation and management (Milner, 1957; Baranger and Baranger, 1966; Langs, 1976). The increasing intrusion of third parties into the treatment setting, however, requires us to reconsider the relationship between these two methods of intervention.

Establishing the framework for an interpretive treatment requires competent management. Once patient and therapist agree on a framework, interpretation can become the principal vehicle for analytic work. With the increased power of third-party payers, however, establishing the frame has been disrupted by difficulties negotiating payment, frequency of appointments, and duration of treatment. Providing a setting for interpretation is yielding to a form of business and behavioral management that primarily attends to resources and symptoms (Halpert, 1972; de Nobel, 1989). This dramatic change has altered the ways in which patients can engage in deepening therapeutic work. For patients with financial resources, traditional psychoanalysis remains available and will continue to provide us with rich ideas about human psychopathology and development. The challenge that faces us is how to apply these ideas with integrity for patients in treatment settings affected by new forms of resource management.

PERSONALITY DISORDERS

A personality disorder is an adaptation an individual makes to an aberrant interpersonal environment, usually the environment of a family (Shapiro et al., 1975). Families create a shared human context to meet the needs of individuals within them. In families whose members have personality disorders, individuals often form rigid defenses against recognizing limitations in themselves, in others, and in available resources (Shapiro, 1982a). These defenses protect them from feelings of helplessness, anxiety, rage, and grief. The price of this protection is the development of rigid or aberrant interpersonal and family boundaries (Shapiro et al., 1975; Shapiro, 1982b). Children's adaptation of their personality structures to fit their experience of these boundaries—no matter how traumatic—is functional. It helps with their emotional survival and supports parents' engagement in some kind of caretaking roles. Adaptation to a constricted family environment does not, however, help develop the child's long-term capacity to grapple flexibly and creatively with the ever-changing reality outside the family.

The world does not conform to the individual's needs. In response, the so-called personality-disordered person displays what the DSM-IV calls "an enduring pattern of inner experience and behavior that deviates markedly from the expectations of the individual's culture." This pattern represents an effort by the individual to change the world into a familiar place (Shapiro and Carr, 1991). Limitations in the world—impassible boundaries marked by insufficient resources or conflicting needs—can cause the character-disordered individual to become symptomatic. For example, obsessive patients faced with time limitations can become anxious, and narcissistic patients confronting the unavailability of significant people can withdraw or become angry. Clearly defined task and role boundaries in therapy—which help articulate experience so that patients can fully acknowledge it—may allow for a different outcome. These boundaries slow the interactions so that the obsessive can notice how his efforts to control contribute to his anxiety. The narcissist can recognize her need for the other's attention. For patients, experiencing and studying transactions across these therapeutic boundaries offers an opportunity for learning (Bion, 1962). Patients begin to recognize their desperate efforts to change the outside world to fit their needs. With this recognition, they have a chance to gain perspective on their childhood and current maladaptive style and notice that situations in the world require negotiation.

Mental health professionals are in a comparable position. We have grown up in a professional "family" to which we have adapted. Generations of thinkers in dynamic psychiatry have taught us to offer our patients a particular therapeutic setting in the hospital or in the therapeutic dyad. This included time for an externalization of aspects of the patient's personality within the transference. Seeing these externalizations provided an opportunity for the patient to gain perspective on what he or she was trying to repeat or reconfigure. Our increasingly focused interpretive efforts and therapeutic zeal allowed us, with our patients, to extend treatments. Although the individual session was determined by the beginning and end of the hour, psychotherapy itself was without time boundaries. For some, therapy became a way of life, lasting more than a decade. Deep became deeper, with formulations and case reports emerging in the psychoanalytic literature about the recovery and fruitful analysis of infantile, pre-verbal experience. Because our focus was relentlessly inward, we were more likely to overlook the impact of a decade-long intensive therapeutic relationship on our lives and families and those of our patients. For example, to my knowledge, there has been no study of the incidence of therapist or patient divorce following extended psychodynamic work. We decreased our attention to outer-world boundaries—initially noted with the establishment of the frame—in exchange for an extended focus on interpretation.

The outer world has now intruded. For most patients in psychoanalysis, psychotherapy, and hospital care, we can no longer provide this traditional setting. Like our character-disordered patients, we, too, are now facing unanticipated boundaries and limits in the outer world. Psychodynamic therapists had found it difficult to incorporate resource management functions into their settings because of their involvement in the therapeutic process. Insurance companies and managed-care organizations have now taken authority for these functions. As Plaut (1990, p. 310) noted, "that part of common reality which we shut out for the sake of the necessary seclusiveness . . . has a way of reasserting itself." It does not look like we can change this world back into a familiar place. Our difficulty in acknowledging and integrating aspects of the altered external context into our treatment framework may even repeat boundary disturbances characteristic of our patients' families. To maintain our integrity and keep our therapeutic enterprise grounded in reality, we must reexamine the basics of our treatment setting in this new context.

THE FRAMEWORK

Over the years, psychoanalysts have learned to define and manage a therapeutic framework within which a deepening treatment can take place (Milner, 1957; Baranger and Baranger, 1966; Langs, 1973, 1976; Raney, 1982). Milner (1957) noted that the frame has a crucial boundary function, in that it "marks off an area within which what is perceived has to be taken symbolically, while what is outside the frame is taken literally" (p. 158). It is our responsibility to manage this framework, which includes: confidentiality and role boundaries, time, place, setting, financial arrangements, and vacations. We structure these arrangements in the outer world of our contractual negotiation with another adult, who agrees to take up the patient role. We do all of this both to take care of ourselves and to support an interpretive treatment task.

The framework thus has footholds in external reality and in the analytic dyad. For example, we set our fees according to pressures in our outer world, in response to the market and our patients' resources. Fees, vacations, the management of missed sessions—all of the framework issues—are the context within which our patients make sense of us. These structures, therefore, link the developing transference to external-world pressures on both patient and analyst. If the patient's spouse and child require particular vacation times that do not coincide with the analyst's vacation, it raises a framework issue. When the analyst requires the patient to pay for sessions missed during the patient's vacation, it affects the patient's family relations. If the analyst does not charge, the patient's vacation affects the analyst's income and, indirectly, his or her family. Every aspect of framework negotiation is deeply embedded in the inner and outer worlds of both participants.

When patient and analyst negotiate a clearly structured framework, they respectfully address this complexity and provide a safe, predictable, transitional space for therapeutic work. With this security, an individual can take up the patient role and risk a symbolic regression in which an interpretable transference to the analyst can evolve. Though the management structures of the framework quickly enter the patient's inner world of private meaning (Raney, 1982; Rudominer, 1984; Dimen, 1994) and what Ogden calls "the third of the analyst-patient intersubjectivity" (Ogden, 1994), the analyst is responsible for establishing them. The way in which the analyst manages these issues is a reflection of how she manages the boundary between her inner and outer worlds. It, therefore, provides information to her patients about her character (Langs, 1976). The patient's interpretation of the analyst's management is a reflection of the patient's inner world. We meet our patients at this intimate management boundary to engage in the task of interpretive treatment.

The management of the framework and its incorporation into an interpretable transference illuminate the necessary integration in dynamic treatment of management and interpretation. There can be no interpretation without competent management, and no useful management without interpretation. When linked to the shared task of understanding, the two methods—understood psychoanalytically—provide tools for examining the boundary between the patient's inner and outer worlds.

For neurotic patients, the framework is largely a silent aspect of the work. These patients have internalized a stable psychic structure. Patients with severe personality disorders, in contrast, crash against boundaries. Many enter the hospital because of their inability to manage a secure framework for their outside lives. Quite often, it is within and around the framework of treatment that these patients enact their psychopathology. These interactions impinge on therapists at our management boundary, evoking countertransference reactions and framework errors. The study of these mutual enactments has deepened our learning about the fine distinctions between transference and countertransference. In such treatments, our authority for the framework, our ability to manage it, and our commitment to holding the treatment task as primary become crucial.

MANAGEMENT AND INTERPRETATION

Advanced technology has contributed to an increasingly interdependent world. We are more aware both of our needs for others and our limited resources. Institutions that society has counted on to manage dependency—the family, religion, education, health care—have become less dependable. These changes make growing up in this society more difficult and have escalated demands for mental health care. In response, the field has grown enormously. Now that its requirements have threatened to exceed limited resources, its variously trained practitioners have reacted to the pressures with both disarray and rigidity. The therapeutic pair is deeply embedded in a world where there is less time available for sustained intimacy. An intensive, intimate relationship makes powerful demands on both participants. Pressure builds to meet dependency needs instead of interpreting them. We can see the disarray in the increasing number of therapists who have lost their capacity to manage themselves in role. One reaction is for therapists to surrender their management capacities in exchange for a quasi-delusional intimacy manifest in sexual involvement. Alternatively, for some, time boundaries can become irrelevant with the therapeutic grandiosity of an endless treatment.

Another response to the intensity of the work and the limited resources is to develop a defensive, rigid, hyper-management style. Questioning the dangers of interpretive intimacy, many mental health practitioners are turning to the use of prescribed and highly organized management interventions without interpretation. For many practitioners untrained in dynamic thinking, this mode of intervention serves as an adaptive defense against powerful feelings—the patients' and their own—that they can neither tolerate nor understand. However, such prioritization and monitoring of the patient's behavior transforms the semipermeable learning boundaries between therapist and patient into impermeable barriers and risks depleting the treatment of meaning.

In each instance, one aspect of the work is lost: management or interpretation. In each, we move away from the combined interventions that allow for containment and exploration of the patient's inner world. We substitute either the delusion of "oneness" or the safety of arbitrary and rigid management. We fuse with our patients or we direct them. Both responses are defensive substitutes for the risky possibility of learning with them in a transitional space that allows for both empathy and interpretation (Brickman, 1993). Both groups engage in an irrational split where projections and counterprojections flourish. The heartless fiscal manager is no less a projected stereotype than the greedy, self-indulgent clinician.

In the face of this anxiety and splitting, extraordinary changes have taken place. Businesspeople run psychiatric hospitals and have developed new approaches to manage money and institutional survival. Clinical thinking no longer guides institutional life. Even more disturbing is the way that manic defenses have replaced terrified withdrawal. The most sober clinicians are now touting the effectiveness of seven-day treatments for patients with personality disorders. To a certain extent this change represents a course correction from our past avoidance of external reality. However, there is real danger that the power of a genuinely negotiated interpretive understanding of people's lives will be irrevocably lost in the service of managerial efficiency.

At the 1994 meetings of the American Psychiatric Association, I discussed several papers on the treatment of personality disorder in the managed-care era. The papers inevitably focused on short-term interventions into lifelong disorders and offered a range of approaches in response to the current pressures in the field to manage symptoms without interpretation.

One group of authors represented the managers. They discussed the need to focus behavioral and educative interventions in a brief period. One (Silk et al., 1994) described how his staff works effectively with hospitalized borderline patients in seven to fourteen days. The staff advises patients in advance about the time limits and encourages them to have modest goals. Staggered by the rapid turnover and severe patient pathology, staff members benefit from having clearly defined offerings; group and educational sessions help patients by structuring their brief time in the hospital. Patients agree to work on cognitive-behavioral learning, which bolsters their defenses against the feelings of abandonment that lead to their intolerable actions. Silk suggested that a regularly interrupted but essentially long-term relationship with the institution allows patients gradually to recognize and face these feelings. The task of hospitalization is to educate patients about their illness and teach them to manage their symptoms. There is no time for interpretation, and no secure relationship within which one can interpret. Silk does not comment on the possible social implications of setting up a covert managerial system of chronic care. Nor does he consider the possible enactment of a potentially interpretable dynamic of sustained dependency, not unlike that of interminable dynamic treatment.

Another author (Falcon, 1994) assessed this strategy by pooling statistics from Blue Cross/Blue Shield utilization review. Intensive management of mental illness (through constricting hospital stays and duration of treatment) appeared to save a great deal of money. However, when he examined the total expenditures, he found that the costs remained the same, before and after managed care. What had shifted was the accounting of these costs from the psychiatric column to the medical. Patients with mental illness who received no definitive treatment ended up in emergency wards and internists' offices with behavioral and physical manifestations. Management without interpretation seemed to lead to cost shifting without cost saving.

Glen Gabbard (1994) from Menninger spoke in defense of the work of the interpreter. He noted that the artificial limits caused by rigid resource management caused damage to patients working in an interpretive frame. In his studies, borderline patients begin to allow the development of a negative transference at approximately the thirtieth session. This is a customary limit of outpatient resources. Arbitrary interruption at this point was particularly traumatic, as patients regularly experienced it as confirmation of their negative transference, which made it impossible to interpret. Gabbard focused on the need for continuity in the therapeutic relationship, suggesting that a primary task of treatment is to help patients develop a sense of self-continuity over time. Speaking to the necessity for extended treatment, he portrayed resource managers as unwittingly attacking and endangering the patients' treatment. He did not comment on the possibility of integrating the external limits into the therapist's framework.

The differences between managers and interpreters are evocative. Interpreters imply that resource management is destructive and argue for long term treatment. Their therapeutic neutrality gives patients room to take charge of their lives. It may not, however, sufficiently attend to the covert gratifications of interminable treatment for both participants. The passionate argument of interpreters—which gives management little significance—makes it increasingly unlikely that third-party payers will continue to finance this approach.

Managers offer patients coping strategies, frequent short-term admissions, and cognitive schema. Interpretations are irrelevant. Managers use less expensive staff, place patients in groups to study behavior, and prescribe a combination of medication and education. They move people along. Patients treated this way may not take charge of their illness. They may end up receiving nonpsychiatric care that is just as expensive as definitive psychological treatment.

Such management interventions have unexpected side effects for patients with personality disorders. Many of these patients use externalizing defenses, blaming others for what happens to them. In intensive treatment, these patients reveal that behind the externalization lies punitive unconscious self-criticism (Kris, 1990), a phenomenon that leads to their self-destructive behavior. In a treatment environment where managerial experts judge and correct their behavior, show them their vulnerabilities, and teach them "more adaptive" ways to live, these patients readily mobilize this self-criticism. They can interpret a managerial approach as confirmation of their incompetence. In addition, many of these patients have grown up in families where parents believe they know what is going on in the child's mind. They tell the child the way to live rather than helping her discover her own way. This "pathological certainty" (Shapiro, 1982b) contributes to the despairing sense many of these patients have that their ideas, their motivations, and their efforts to understand are of no interest and no value. Managerial therapists may unwittingly contribute to an unproductive repetition of this experience.

Interpreters also run into problems. Gabbard (1991) noted how patient and therapist can join to idealize interpretation and exclude and stereotype the financial manager. This repeats a different familial pattern, in which one parent forms an exclusive dyad with the child, stereotyping and excluding the other parent. The use of the child as an ally interferes with learning and excludes the third party necessary for grappling with reality. Collusive pairing between therapist and patient in an endless treatment is problematic. It can conceal a shared hatred of limitations, a fantasy of endless resources, and a delusional dyadic structure.

Bion (1961) described the shared irrationality inherent in any "pairing" disconnected from the larger group's task. The notion of an isolated dyad, however, is an illusion. The therapeutic pair has always been embedded in a larger context: the community, the profession, the managed-care networks, the mental institution. Though we do not always pay attention to this, there is inevitably a "third" that keeps the pair grounded in reality.

There is increasing interest within the analytic literature in the notion of "the third." Abelin (1971) wrote about early triangulation and the function of the father for both mother and child in protecting the pair from being overwhelmed with symbiosis. Lacan (1975) developed the idea of the symbolic third ("le nom du père") as a function that grounds the individual in a larger context. Brickman (1993) described interpretation as a third factor facilitating separation from therapeutic symbiosis, and Ogden (1994) described "the third" factor of the analyst-patient intersubjectivity.

Though the issues differ, these notions are applicable to the external third of the managed-care reviewer and insurance company. In the childhood triad, the father shares the same task as the mother-infant dyad: facilitating the child's development. The payer's task, however, is different from that of the therapy pair: financial management, not treatment. But these latter two tasks are linked: both financial management and treatment require attention to the reality of limitations.

Inevitably, the patient brings external parties into the relationship and incorporates them into the interpretive space. This is a familiar phenomenon of psychodynamic work (Schafer, 1985). It is not just the patient, however, who introduces third-party resource managers. These agencies bring pressures to bear on both members of the dyad in ways that affect the therapist's capacity to focus on the patient's experience. The therapist must come to terms with them to undertake the work and to clarify what "the work" can be, given the limitations.

Focusing on the dyad, Freud once referred to the patient's family as "an external resistance to treatment" (Freud, 1917). Some have argued (Langs, 1973; Raney, 1982) that managed-care providers constitute such a powerful external resistance that interpretive treatment is impossible. Others disagree (Rudominer, 1984; de Nobel, 1989). No matter the source, patients struggle with these external third parties over available resources and interpret that struggle according to their own psychopathology. Therapists can use these struggles as a part of the treatment, if they can find a way to take in the external limitations as an aspect of their treatment frame.

Patients with personality disorders chronically repeat problematic behavior. These repetitions, however, are more than self-destructive enactments. They are also desperate efforts to learn something new, to gain perspective on an unconscious process. When the patient's experience is not conscious and is enacted through dangerous behavior, a safe space within a secure frame is essential. A secure framework represents a negotiated reality that incorporates the limitation of resources. For many patients, third-party managers represent an aspect of that reality. If the therapist can incorporate this external factor into the framework, she can help her patient understand the transference meaning of these limitations and how such meaning has governed his behavior in the past or governs it in the present.

AN INSTITUTIONAL MODEL

The Austen Riggs Center has developed a management structure that brings together financial people and clinicians to address the framework for treatment. Limitation of resources is both reality and metaphor. Patients, staff, family, and insurer share the reality: they must recognize and manage it. The metaphor requires discovery and interpretation. Our effort has been to bring the patient and family into the financial discussions between the hospital and the external third party. This allows them to examine their assumptions regarding the need for treatment and the limitations of resources. The process eventually authorizes the patient to speak and act as the critical agent of change. Inevitably, the patient's reactions to limitations reflect a character-driven response to frustration and illuminate repetitive dynamic themes. Excluding patients from this experience or confusing them by discounting or devaluing the financial managers deprives them of an opportunity for speaking as well as learning.

Eric Plakun (1994) from Riggs has described how a patient's mother continually rescued him—both emotionally and financially—from taking charge of his life. She repeatedly bailed him out when he overextended himself. In the hospital, when the insurance coverage was about to end, the patient's behavior worsened. He requested a rate reduction from the hospital to stay longer. The financial officer was inclined to agree. In the clinical-financial discussion, the clinical staff recognized and interpreted to the patient the repetition of his family dynamic, with the hospital in the role of mother. He saw how he was enacting a lifelong pattern of inviting his mother's overprotective response. He began to see his pattern of blaming his mother for her overprotectiveness while demanding through regression that she continue to meet his needs. The discussion led to a decision by the patient to step down to a less expensive program. He obtained a job to support the program and negotiated a small reduction from the hospital and a contribution from his mother. Through the staff's integration of management and interpretation, the patient could begin to take charge of the conflict.

With the help of this interdisciplinary structure, we invite patients to take responsibility for making moves to less expensive settings in our system. Facing their own financial limitations, they initiate requests for transition rather than allowing others to move them. Stimulated by pressures from insurance companies, managed-care firms, or families, our patients frequently resist assuming authority for these moves. The clinical staff works with them toward articulating their resistance within the developing transference. Feelings of abandonment, neglect, and abuse regularly recur. The therapist, with the help of the institution, attempts to mediate these pressures and feelings with the patient, sustaining the reality limitation and placing the feelings within an interpretive context.

Grief often results. With this working link between clinical and financial thinking, patient, family, and staff have an opportunity to learn from their shared irrationality about limits. In this setting, the negotiated management of limitations becomes the framework for interpretation.

It is possible in a short period, even with disturbed patients, to develop collaborative dynamic interpretation of these reactions. The therapist must, however, incorporate the reality of limitations into his framework and interpret within that space. When therapist and patient develop a shared recognition that resources are limited, the patient often directs his rage at the therapist as representative of that reality. Working through this rage leads to grief, mourning, and a genuinely intimate engagement around treatment and its limitations. For example, an adopted patient had lost his biological father at an early age and did not get along with his new father. Throughout his life he had been beaten by his stepfather when he could not perform. Unable to provide help or recognize his stepson's need for him, the older man would strike him. This patient gradually developed a characterologic adaptation to challenges, oscillating between helpless vulnerability with wishes for idealized rescue and aggressive grandiosity. The vulnerability reflected his need for a loving father, the grandiosity, his angry effort to manage everything himself. When faced with a task, he thus unconsciously evoked his relationship with his stepfather. He needed help in seeing the pattern, tolerating the experience, and putting it in perspective so that he could increase his choices (Semrad, 1969). This patient was overwhelmed by his fear of his wish to rely on a man. Without containment and interpretation, he could not allow himself to recognize and identify with a man's strength, vulnerability, and competence to become his own man. He needed help to separate from his past.

This patient was hospitalized because of a decompensation around losing his job. Enacting his defensive character solution, he did not hire a lawyer to represent him. He grandiosely took up his own defense and ended up feeling battered by the complexities of the case. In the hospital, he wanted the institution to take his side in court. A success would provide the resources for the long-term treatment he needed. As it stood, he had resources only for short-term treatment. The repetition was familiar. The patient wanted the therapist (as the idealized father) magically to help him get the resources he needed for a better developmental solution. Any failure to respond meant abandonment. When the therapist noted that they only had a short time to work together, it provided a reality boundary. With this, the patient could experience and begin to interpret his negative transference. He saw the therapist as a bad father, who was "knocking him down" without helping him develop his "inadequate resources." With the recognition of a familiar rage, he could begin to see his terror of turning himself over to his therapist for what the therapist had realistically available—treatment, not legal advice. This recognition freed him sufficiently to allow the therapist to define with him an achievable goal. In a brief stay, this patient could learn enough about his terror of relying on a man so that he could dare to hire an effective lawyer to represent him.

DISCUSSION

A familiar and painful life experience for patients with personality disorders is the lack of resources in their families and their lives to ease their emotional development. They have shaped their characters to deny this fact. Managed care—as metaphor—represents this experience. In establishing a treatment setting in which patients can address these issues, therapists must face the changes in our world caused by the limitations of resources. The third-party reviewer—no matter how untrained or clumsy—is the representative of that reality. We must integrate their perspectives into our own framework to provide a safe transitional space in which the patient can risk an interpretable transference.

These third parties—insurance companies or families—often do not make their limitations clear. In such cases, they represent not a well-delineated reality, but an uncertain, chaotic, and unresponsive resource. This, too, is the way of the world, but its impact on dynamic treatment can be devastating. Patient and clinician feel they have no boundaries, no security, no resting place. Clinicians can respond to this relentless ambiguity as an attack on their efforts to provide a safe space for treatment. A defensive response, however, interferes with the possibility of providing either management or interpretation for the patient. Both patient and clinician become incompetent and despairing. This was the experience for one patient, who wrote:

> I'm confused about everything. Should I stay or should I go? I'm so ambivalent and apathetic, it's making any decision impossible. It was my assumption that I'd come to the hospital, cut to the chase, as it were, and concentrate on intensive therapy. But the insurance company has made that quite impossible. I don't have a clue when they'll say, "You're out of here," so I had a mind set to go home this week because I thought they'd kick me out. Talk about undermining any work to be done. So now that I'm in this mind set, I want to go home. It has become more appealing the more I've thought about it. That's tough though, because the stuff makes me feel so bad and I sure don't want to go to school with all this dredged up shit making me feel bad. . . . The insurance company is also making me feel really uprooted here and since I know I'm going home before school anyway, I might feel more settled by moving home. . . . I've been living on the edge for more or less eight years, so I personally don't see the difference where I am. Home, school, hospital. Now it's all the same. Because I couldn't get what I wanted out of hospital and that was my last resource. So I'll just have to keep doing what I've been doing.

Even in these cases, however, the therapist can manage a dynamic intervention if she holds to her interpretive task. The recognition that patients with personality disorder regularly use aspects of the frame for enacting a repetitive theme is central. With our help, they can use this experience to discover their metaphor. The patient does not initially experience his or her behavior as either repetition or metaphor. Grasping the metaphor, however, is itself a shift toward recognizing and stopping the repetition. For this patient, her suicidal depression and isolation stemmed from the disruption of her family in early adolescence. During this period, her family was unpredictable and chaotic, intermittently absent, and confusing. She had to take charge of her life alone, with resulting despair. In the face of the managed-care response, this patient could see how she chose a familiar interpretation for a more complex reality. The third-party reviewer was, like her parents, confused, uncertain, and not attending to her needs. However, the therapist, who had incorporated this reality, was available to her to make sense of this, both as reality and as transference. Choosing the familiar and devastating chaos as the reason for her despair was this patient's repetition. The overwhelming repetition of childhood confusion did not allow her to discover her adult perspective and resources. With a stable focus on the interpretive task within this framework, she could recognize this and choose from more complex options.

The title of this chapter is "The Boundaries Are Shifting: Renegotiating the Therapeutic Frame." I suspect that this apparent shift in framework boundaries and our pressure to redefine and renegotiate them is both reality and illusion. The confusion derives from our anxious uncertainty about the future and our reluctance to see how we have contributed to the development of systems of external management. As John Muller (1994) has noted, "If the contemporary rush toward the dyad in our theories has served to eclipse the place we give [the] third, one possible outcome is to leave the field vacant for an unwelcome intruder. The place of the third . . . has been seized by the managed care [provider, who] . . . structures the dyadic process from first to last, determines its semiotic conditions, influences what is to be said or not said, [and] dictates what shall be taken as meaningful and what shall be desired as an outcome."

I suggest that if we hold to the essence of our frame, we have a chance to ride out this storm. We can continue to provide our patients with definable structures for interpreting their lives if we can help them manage sufficient resources for even the beginnings of an interpretive space. Then, we may rediscover how competent management and reliably negotiated interpretation are inextricably linked in the provision of dynamic treatment.

I should like to thank Drs. Donna Elmendorf, M. Gerard Fromm, John Muller, Elizabeth Oakes, and James Sacksteder for their helpful comments on an earlier draft of this paper.

REFERENCES

Abelin, E. L. (1971). The role of the father in separation-individuation. In *Separation-Individuation: Essays in Honor of Margaret Mahler*, ed. J. McDevitt and C. Settlage. New York: International Universities Press, pp. 229–252.

Baranger, M., and W. Baranger. (1966). Insight in the analytic situation. In *Psychoanalysis in the Americas*, ed. R. Litman. New York: International Universities Press, pp. 56–72.

Bion, W. R. (1961). *Experiences in Groups*. London: Tavistock.

——. (1962). Learning from experience. In *Seven Servants*. New York: Aronson, 1977.

Brickman, H. R. (1993). "Between the devil and the deep blue sea": The dyad and the triad in psychoanalytic thought. *International Journal of Psychoanalysis*, 74:905–915.

De Nobel, L. (1989). When it is not the patient who pays. *Psychoanalytic Psychotherapy*, 4:1–12.

Dimen, M. (1994). "Money, love and hate: contradiction and paradox in psychoanalysis. *Psychoanalytic Dialogues*, 4:69–100.

Falcon, S. (1994). Finances and insurance. Presented at the annual meeting of the American Psychiatric Association.

Freud, S. (1917). Introductory lectures on psychoanalysis. *Standard Edition*, 16:448–463.

Gabbard, G. (1991) A psychodynamic perspective on the clinical impact of insurance review. *American Journal of Psychiatry*, 148:318–323.

——. (1994). Character disorder in the managed care era. Presented at the annual meeting of the American Psychiatric Association.

Halpert, E. (1972). The effect of insurance on psychoanalytic treatment. *Journal of the American Psychoanalytic Association*, 20:122–133.

Kris, A. (1990). Helping patient by analysing self-criticism. *Journal of the American Psychoanalytic Association*, 38:605–636.

Lacan, J. (1975). *The Seminar: Book I*. Cambridge: Cambridge University Press. (1988).

Langs, R. (1973). *The Technique of Psychoanalytic Psychotherapy*. New York: Aronson.

——. (1976). *The Bipersonal Field*. New York: Aronson.

Milner, M. (1957). *On Not Being Able to Paint*. New York: International Universities Press.

Muller, J. (1994). Intersubjectivity through semiotics: Why sound bites won't do. Unpublished manuscript.

Ogden, T. H. (1994). The analytical third: Working with intersubjective clinical facts. *International Journal of Psycho-analysis*, 75:3–20.

Plakun, E. (1994). The clinical-financial interface: A novel strategy. Presented at the annual meeting of the American Psychiatric Association.

Plaut, A. (1990). The presence of the third: Intrusive factors in analysis. *Journal of Analytical Psychology*, 35:301–315.

Raney, J. O. (1982). The payment of fees for psychotherapy. *International Journal of Psychoanalytic Psychotherapy*, 9:147–181.

Rudominer H. S. (1984). Peer review, third party payment, and the analytic situation: A case report. *Journal of the American Psychoanalytic Association*, 32:773–795.

Schafer, R. (1985). The interpretation of psychic reality, developmental influences, and unconscious communication. *Journal of the American Psychoanalytic Association*, 33:537–554.

Semrad, E. (1969). *Teaching Psychotherapy of Psychotic Patients*. New York: Grune and Stratton.

Shapiro, E. R. (1982a). The holding environment and family therapy with acting out adolescents. *International Journal of Psychoanalytic Psychotherapy*, 9:209–226.

———. (1982b). On curiosity: Intrapsychic and interpersonal boundary formation in family life. *International Journal of Family Psychiatry*, 3:69–89.

Shapiro, E. R., and A. W. Carr. (1991). *Lost in Familiar Places: Creating New Connections between the Individual and Society*. New Haven and London: Yale University Press.

Shapiro, E. R., J. Zinner, R. L. Shapiro, and D. A. Berkowitz. (1975). The influence of family experience on borderline personality development. *International Review of Psychoanalysis*, 2:399–411.

Silk, K., et al. (1994). Short-term hospitalization. Presented at the annual meeting of the American Psychiatric Association.

Roy Schafer

■ 2 Conformity and Individualism

Any therapist who works within the framework of psychoanalytic understanding will not take the terms *conformity* and *individualism* at face value—that is, as these terms are commonly used to describe overt social conduct. Those patients who, at first glance, seem to fit neatly into one of these categories usually prove, on close examination, to be far more complex inwardly than they seem. The therapist will want to understand why conformity or individualism has figured so prominently in a person's social life or persona, when that is the case, and whether or how either of these plays a significant role in the suffering that has brought the patient to treatment.

I believe that the average well-trained and well-analyzed therapist can set aside his or her own values sufficiently in this respect to be able to approach the patient with a mind open enough to get the job done. In other words, in this context, therapists can approximate the analytic model of neutrality, equidistance from the constituents of conflict, and consistent control of disruptive countertransferential tendencies. On that basis they are prepared to understand clinical instances of pronounced social conformity and individualism and in each instance conduct treatment reasonably and effectively.

After presenting an analytic-descriptive account of these two extremes, I shall present some brief summaries of work with specific patients. Then, in the discussion section, I shall return to qualify in one important respect this puristic analytic model of work with the extremes of social conformity and individualism. That qualification will lead us into both technical issues and questions about the nature of our knowledge of the world around us.

CONFORMITY

Conformity contributes to the appearance of having identity. This is so not only in the minds of witnesses but also in each conformist's conscious experience. Continuous steadiness of conformist conduct may come to seem so natural to the conformist that it occasions none of the "Who am I?" sorts of questions with which many people plague themselves. Those who pursue this conformist course are likely to be already extremely turned off to and, so, turned away from, the ambiguities of their inner worlds. Their conscious experience is focused on simplistic versions of what goes on around them and how to fit into it unobtrusively. They keep busy judging how closely they approximate common features of the surrounding world. By blocking impulsive actions that may carry marks of individuality they hope to escape critical scrutiny by others. Their motto is "No surprises." In its way, conformity also tends to control others, for it can make them, too, self-conscious about being different.

Notwithstanding those efforts to achieve identity through a kind of anonymity, these conformists remain exposed to indiscriminate experiences of shame. They are embarrassed whenever they judge that they have lapsed from being acceptably expectable and unremarkable. Shame, one might say, is the main affect signal by which they regulate their conduct and conscious experience. Being turned so much to the outside world as they view it, they steadily impoverish further their already severely restricted conscious experience of their inner worlds. They shrink their potential for using inner life creatively in work, love, and play. Indeed, being shamed also seems to have been a major feature of their experiences as children—enough so that the development of organized, relatively autonomous superego functioning and its derivatives in moral codes seem to have been retarded. Thus, they can also be secret transgressors to a surprising degree, and they live with a fear of discovery.

On deeper levels of experience and unconscious fantasy, this artificially naturalized conformity is built on rubble. So it seems upon the analysis that may become possible during those not rare occasions when some degree of decompensation afflicts the conformist. Extreme conformity seems then to be built over fragmented selves and objects, lack of purpose and sense of agency, an intolerance of ambiguity and pain so great that it precludes emotional commitment to individualized others and sets severe limitations on the sense of aliveness. Using the defenses of splitting, denial, idealization, and projective identification of what they cannot tolerate in themselves, extreme conformists empty themselves of individuality. They constantly try to put an end to spontaneous, unrehearsed, unscrutinized expressions of feeling and flights of imagination.

The functioning of these conformists features blocked incorporation of whatever they find around them that seems obviously individual and so could tempt them toward experiencing their fragmentation or daring to build an individuality of their own. Supplementing that blocking are persecutory attitudes toward that which they exclude and project. Not only do they throw out the baby with the bath water, they do in the baby that we, as therapists, recognize as their own repudiated selves. In short, these extreme conformists seem to be fully situated in what Melanie Klein (1948) designated the paranoid-schizoid position of psychological development and mode of psychological function. Fundamentally, their ethos is narcissistic, and their thinking is concrete or earthbound.

Extreme conformists are not likely to show up in the office of a dynamic psychotherapist or psychoanalyst. They tend to bring their emotional difficulties to the office of their GP or a medical or surgical specialist, especially when, as is often the case, due to excessive repression these difficulties are expressed mostly psychosomatically. As a last resort they prefer to turn to a drug-oriented and supportive general psychiatrist. But if, somehow, they turn up in the office of a therapist who focuses on inner-world experience, they are initially quite uncomprehending, and they give every appearance of seeming to want neither self-understanding nor the experience of being understood, as described so well by Betty Joseph (1983). Traditional Freudians might say of them that they are so well and rigidly defended that their prospects as analysands are not favorable; at best, they may make only limited gains. But no matter what the exploratory therapist's school of thought, he or she will recognize in these suffering conformists a great vulnerability to panic should the depths of their inner world ever be opened up to them without extensive preparatory work.

Sometimes therapy can help extreme conformists get beyond the panic and the defenses that surround it. In a slow and zigzag way and over a long period of time, exploratory treatment may make a big difference in their psychological status and further development. These patients may become able to confront their hostile introjects consciously and with some confidence that they will be able to contain them; they may get to know firsthand their vulnerable, fragmented, fluid, and despairing selves, their dreadfully low self-esteem, and their deep-seated feelings of shame, emptiness, and vulnerability. They may be convinced that they have lived in a world characterized by being persecuted or by persecuting others. In short, they may begin to explore their Kafkaesque inner world and define ways out of it.

I have been describing prominent trends that one may expect to encounter in the treatment of those who are, relatively speaking, extreme conformists. They are hypothetically pure cases. In life, we encounter all degrees of emphasis on this mode of adjustment. (I leave aside for the moment the benevolent, growth-enhancing aspects of conformity without panic.) Consequently, the therapist or analyst should not be misled by constricted self-presentations into foreclosing the possibility that therapy will reveal as yet hidden enclaves of individuality. Like patched-up chinks in armor, these enclaves may offer entries into the psychic retreats described by John Steiner (1993). Then these flaws can be turned to good advantage, given adequate patience and tact on the therapist's part.

No single interpretive line is guaranteed to be helpful in every case or throughout the work with any one patient. There is, however, one aspect of too-conformist patients that has often seemed to me to be useful in finding a way to approach them, and that is their need to avoid surprises and keep excitement to a minimum. Often, it is obviously the surprise or excitement of romantic or erotic feelings or both, and sometimes the surprise or excitement of indignation or other forms of critical or angry engagement with others. In both cases, there will be complex issues to sort out and try to work through. Frequently, however, the prospects of surprise or excitement reside simply in exposure to novelty or the adventurous possibilities of travel or a change of residence or job, or they may reside in unexpectedly rewarding experiences with others such as enthusiastic praise.

As usual, the transference is a likely place to pick up signs of the struggle against excitement and surprise. And it is there that these patients may do their damnedest to remain disengaged—or at least to seem so. They hope thereby to deny the therapist the pertinent cues. Here, identification and exploration of this policy of control through remoteness may show that excitement and surprise are (unconsciously or consciously) equated with chaos, flooding, complete loss of control, or rapid spilling over into disastrous action, all leading to the debacle of personal fragmentation and humiliation at the hands of the therapist. Anal prototypes are likely to dominate these expectations. For example, surprises may be fantasized as the so-called accidents of bowel training; they are mess-making. Orgasm itself may be a terrible anal explosion.

One way these patients show their dread during treatment is by rapidly appending mention of actual or possible negative aspects to whatever unexpected positive experience enters into their associations and then dwelling on the negative to the exclusion of the positive. For example, a good feeling about the preceding session may have to be disparaged at length as being defensive, superficial, or too compliant. Or, if surprised by indignation, they will shrug off the feeling because they know "the rules of treatment," or they really think the therapist is, if anything, "too kind" or just being "a bit provocative" for their good. Similarly, if proud of themselves, they are sure that they will let this "boasting" go to their heads and ruin everything. Altogether, they resemble severe governesses keeping children under constant critical surveillance and using pinches, frowns, and chilly tones to maintain or restore order.

Understandably, anything approaching free association is initially intolerable. It is avoided, or simulated by nonstop talking or using prepared agendas or constantly contriving painful crises in their daily lives that give them lots to talk about in the sessions.

Throughout this struggle, a therapist can recognize that a sense of omnipotence is being confirmed by the maintenance of iron control of the self and others, including control of the therapist. The composure of conventionality is a powerful weapon of the righteous in their never-ending struggle against the "perverse," "vulgar," "evil," "alien" forces in the world, of which the therapist may become, in the transference and through projective identification, the chief representative.

INDIVIDUALISM

Turning to the other hypothetically pure case, that of extreme individualism, one may find that, below the surface, things are much the same as with the extreme conformists. In certain important respects, some things may even be similar on the surface. When it is extreme, a deliberate policy of individualism implies a horror of conformity, however that person represents it, and so it is constantly defining itself by what it must not be—what Erikson (1956) called negative identity. Thus, it is not so much otherness that is being constructed by these individualists; their goal is the construction of oppositeness as a steady state. When it is genuine and relaxed, otherness or alterity opens a near-infinity of possibilities, including selective conformities without panic. In contrast, the extreme individualist, having adopted a posture that may be strikingly counterphobic or rebellious or some of both, is self-defining under severe constraints. The premises of this position are embodied in the unconscious fantasies it enacts, and they are those of the paranoid-schizoid position as described for the conformists: fragmentation of self and objects and all the rest. And, like the conformists, they live in a predominantly narcissistic internal ethos.

In these instances, however, there is likely to be more unconscious emphasis on fantasies of omnipotence. Whatever analytic treatment is possible will show this to be so. These extreme individualists are enacting a way of being totally self-originating, in effect imagining themselves as androgynous gods giving birth to themselves. Socially, they may strike stereotypical poses derived from nineteenth-century Romanticism, as though they are so "original" that nothing they do or feel has any precedent whatsoever. These poses come across to the knowledgeable as parodies or mere gestures of imaginativeness and freedom. To maintain their illusions of omnipotence, they cannot allow themselves to respect tradition and to draw on it to help them work toward change, as a self-confident creative person might. Nor can they draw on inner-world experience to put a convincing personal stamp on what they do. Defined as they are by negativity and grandiosity, they must try to fabricate on demand an inner world and an outer form for it, the result being that their subjectivity will be considered theatrical and shallow by all but the naive.

Expectably, these patients fear treatment and fight it desperately. They are notoriously difficult to treat owing to their pronounced narcissistic personality organization and its dependence on omnipotence fantasies. A variety of therapeutic approaches has been presented in the clinical literature (see, e.g., Kernberg, 1975); however, none of them has been universally accepted. Presumably, the outcome in each case depends on the unique pairing of therapist and patient and the severity of the disorder.

CONFORMITY, INDIVIDUALISM, AND IDENTITY

Taking the extremes of conformity and individualism together, I suggest that they represent two kinds of what have been called false selves (Winnicott, 1958). But we must also allow falseness a quantitative aspect—a position on a continuum rather than a fixed, absolute, and even discontinuous position.

Genuineness in human existence is always at risk. This perspective on risk is consequential for understanding individualistic and conformist identities. Using as a model Erikson's (1956) idea of identity diffusion at one extreme and premature foreclosure at the other—roughly corresponding to what I have been presenting as the extremes of individualism and conformity, respectively—we can say that what lies between them is not so much stable identity (or the cohesive self of Kohut's [1977] theory) as identity that is always at risk. Erikson recognized this to be so. Identity at risk implies acceptance of there being no final resting place and a great need to tolerate ambiguity, tension, and deferral of closure. It also implies the value of maintaining both a heightened realistic sense of continually making choices and a readiness to recenter one's point of view or allow it to be altogether decentered for indefinite periods of time.

All of this characterizes those who live their lives in a manner that is lively and engaged, even if troubled or unsettled. For times and mores do change, fervent beliefs lose their support, some old relationships are no longer supportable, new opportunities wax while old ones wane, and some preferred pleasure possibilities must change with age and circumstance and the surrounding ethos. I believe it is fitting in this regard to speak of a democratization of selfhood or personhood.

None of the foregoing is intended to deny the powerful influence of unconscious mental processes. In principle if not in practice, psychoanalytic therapies can always trace the formative role played by these archaic unconscious processes in whatever is chosen, whatever is changed, and how it is changed; even flexibility or adaptability has its personal-emotional history. It is the singular richness of the psychoanalytic approach to show this continuity within flux. And this flux and this continuity will be defined variously in keeping with the principles of each school of psychoanalytic thought. Each school, however, will maintain a focus on continuity between, on the one hand, the present and, on the other, infantile, unconsciously maintained wishes, defenses, and prohibitions and the fantasies in which they play themselves out. This self-sameness need not be unmistakably evident on the surface of things. It is, however, conspicuous in the results of projective tests before and after effective therapies (Schafer, 1967), and certainly conspicuous in second and even third personal analyses. This deep-down conformity is not that of the mass as viewed by the sociological eye. This is remaining true to lifelong principles of creating experiences of any kind at all.

CLINICAL ILLUSTRATIONS

I shift here to clinical analytic constructions of the following familiar sort. One patient had adjusted early in life to a mother whom he experienced as unable to tolerate the strong needs and demands of others, including himself. He was to be no trouble. If he were, she would shut down emotionally to the point where he would end up feeling abandoned and painfully alone, and perhaps frightened as well. In later life, he tried his best never to be any trouble, meanwhile harboring intense resentment mixed with guilt over this state of affairs. He read this demand that he be no trouble into every relationship, including, of course, the transference relationship. He did so either apprehensively or with conviction that often was based on extreme interpretation of single signs that his presence or conduct was in the least unsettling to the other.

In the context of this chapter, his adjustment can be called an extreme conformism in a world constructed on his mother's terms as these were originally interpreted and applied by him as a child. It was his world, his psychic reality, and there was no saying no to it except indirectly through expectable symptoms, bad moods, and occasional outbursts filled with fear and remorse. As he changed during his treatment, he never forsook this psychic reality, but he did enlarge it to include the possibility of some reality testing and consequently some moderation of anxiety and guilt-proneness. On this basis, he could include a greater range of choice and opportunities for gratification than had been possible before. All of these changes could be seen as moving away from a specialized conformity and toward individualism; alternatively, they could be characterized as demonstrating noteworthy democratization of his personhood.

I do not say democratization of the self, because my entire argument points toward a personhood that is always in flux and that is negotiated and sometimes negated in important respects, and thus is always at risk. I am pointing toward a set of self-processes rather than a monolithic, static self, a once-and-for-all self that precludes deep change. Elsewhere (1992), in a critique of essentialist theories of unitary selves, I have called what I have in mind multiple self-narratives.

Another patient had learned to conform to a pathologically individualistic mother who had abandoned her own conventional social, religious, cultural, and political background and gone to an opposite extreme of what she took to be unconventionality. The patient, who continued into her adult years adoring an idealized fantasy of this mother, had been living a willful existence, adhering very little to what she took to be social convention. In her latency period, however, she had gone through a period of valuing what was clean, orderly, devout, prim, and controlled.

Analytic treatment showed that, with the advent of adolescence, the emphases of this rule-governed period had been deeply repressed and reacted against with the programmatic oppositeness that I mentioned above. It took years of treatment before the quality and importance of this preadolescent period emerged. Once it did emerge, she and I were necessarily engaged with her repeated defensive efforts to ward it off, but we also struggled to find a way to include and represent this one constituent of a complex, viable personhood. In this instance, democratization meant that she no longer wished to be so powerfully exclusive and persecutory of any kind of social conformity.

I have avoided using the word *integrate* and have settled on the word *include* in order not to idealize what is usually accomplished in psychoanalytic therapies. Inclusion of the intrapsychically forbidden, as those who have been treated analytically or practice that kind of treatment know all too well, is a major accomplishment. In this case, this inclusion of conformity took place with no significant compromise of the patient's individualistic spontaneity and creativity, but with continuous unrest about the change.

In another case, a man's individualism took the form of political radicalism with so strong an emphasis on egalitarianism that it covered and rationalized masochistic pleasures; it also served as a reaction formation against wishes to be and fantasies of being a tycoon. In his case, he had to call all self-interest "bourgeois decadence" to stave off the tycoon fantasy.

As a fourth clinical instance, I mention a series of men with whom I have worked whose mothers were more or less severely depressed during their childhood years. Expectably, their ways of constructing their world and their experiences and their personhood, so far as they were able to, had been deeply influenced by what we may call in this regard their failed mothers. As adults, they conformed with terror to the psychic reality that they steadily re-created and projected into the surround. Objectifying this mother was strictly prohibited, and the same was true of the father, who, knowingly or not, had conspired with her to maintain an idealized image of her in the family. He, too, could not be scrutinized freely. This blocking of perception was a deeply entrenched characteristic of these men. Thus idealized and protected, the mother or her surrogates and, secondarily, the father and his surrogates became constant sources of guilt. Need, frustration, and the surprises of spontaneity were strictly forbidden and severely punishable through various forms of mental and physical self-injury. Punishment included repeatedly forming painful though also sadistic relationships with women.

I want to emphasize the attack on reality-testing functions. As in the stereotype of the extreme conformist, severe limitation of content and severe, though selective, impairment of function in all relations with reality were required. Although vocational achievements were not blocked, they had to occur far from personal, intimate human relationships.

This consequence could be seen clearly in the transference relationships these men constructed and the desperation they experienced when they began to face alternatives. Outwardly, each of these men did not give the impression of being unusually conformist. This impression could be attributed in part to inhibitions with regard to observing certain social and sexual conventions, in part to perverse inclinations, in part to counterphobic gestures, and so on. Inwardly, however, they lived the kind of lives that I described in an earlier publication on prisoner fantasies (1983). They were captives in a well-guarded, regimented world in which they had learned to love as well as hate their chains.

In presenting these cases I wanted to show the complexity of conformity and individualism once one departs from a social viewpoint that relies on conduct and consciousness and enters into the depths of the inner world. For there are conformist individuality and specialized conformity in the inner world. Inwardly, each patient emerges in certain profound ways as both extremely conformist and extremely individualistic, and therefore always presents a challenge to the therapist's skills and range.

DISCUSSION

These remarks pave the way for my return to the question of relative immunity from countertransference disruption in the therapies of cases of the sort I have been discussing. The crucial area to consider in this regard is not the patient's usual stance relative to social customs or mores. Rather, it is the patient's usually unconscious stance relative to the therapist's own expectations and needs in his or her professional practice. Patients engaged in intensive treatments develop transferences that focus on these expectations and needs of their therapists, and they try to lure them into enactments in which, as a form of countertransference, the therapists take the part of one side of an internal conflict by assuming the role of one fragment of self or one internalized object. For example, therapists may end up acting in ways that support unconscious fantasies of cruel or negligent parents or despised parts of the self. And patients often succeed in this effort to enact and reenact, even if not to an extent that is certain to wreck the therapy. They may stir up impatience, induce some distractedness, occasion feelings of despair, stimulate moralizing or inappropriate reassurance.

Some therapists have major expectations and needs for positive rapport, based perhaps on strong reparative tendencies, and, unconsciously, they develop strategies for avoiding feeling like bad mothers or fathers. They do not tolerate negative transferences well, especially when these involve sadistic elements. And if they are too easily alarmed by suggestions of even minimal departures from sanity, as they define it, based perhaps on their own family prototypes of madness that they still fear they have incorporated and not fully mastered, they will discourage regressive shifts. They may do this by too readily becoming structuring auxiliary egos who dispense advice or interpretations too soon and too anxiously. Thus, they enforce a kind of conformity to *them* that blocks out important communications of deep-seated problems.

Annie Reich (1951) described these expectations and needs of therapists as characterological countertransferences, that is, as readiness for countertransference not specific to any one patient or situation. These countertransferences are rooted in the reasons one becomes a therapist in the first place. Probably they remain always somewhat active, for good as well as for bad, even after the therapist has undergone the most thorough, effective personal analysis. No one changes totally, especially not on those deep levels. It is those characterological countertransferences that are the roots of our special skills, but they can also be enforcers of strong conformity or pronounced individualism. In this way, they can become sources of trouble in the treatment situation. We all know fellow trainees and colleagues who are prone to depart from neutrality, equidistance, and self-awareness in one or another of these directions, and we all know of flagrant excesses.

We should not be surprised or downhearted by this recognition. As far back as Freud, and contrary to certain official, conformity-inducing denials, these differences among therapists have played their part in theoretical and technical debates in our field. It has been reported that Freud was compelled at one point to emphasize with respect to rigidities creeping into the ideas and practices of his followers, "I am not a Freudian!" Taking a long view, these debates have been profitable; in the short run, however, excessive claims and overheated practices have done much mischief, especially in the treatments of women, gays, and lesbians who have been pressured toward conformity with gender stereotypes.

I center on countertransference in my discussion section to call attention to theoretical and technical overconformity and overindividualism and to lead into my major qualification of my point in the introduction about therapists approximating sufficiently the ideal of neutrality to be able to work well with patients who present these tendencies to excess.

I am a strong believer in the value of looking at psychoanalytic therapy as a dialogue. The dialogue generates the phenomena of the treatment and their interpretation, what I call their tellings and retellings in actions as well as words (1992). Therapy is, in this sense, co-authored. The points of view or values of both therapist and patient will not only set the criteria for what will be regarded as conformity and individualism, but will also limit or facilitate the importance of phenomena thus defined. I believe that all of our descriptions and interpretations, including my own, should be regarded as provisional; if they hold at all, they hold within a perspective or school of thought, such as the Freudian or Kleinian, and they hold among those who demonstrably, even if not totally, share the perspective in question. On this basis, when those who share one perspective look, they can see the same thing; when they speak, they can understand one another; and when they argue, they do not as a rule seem incoherent to one another. One could say they belong to therapeutic subcultures, which means that they abide by most of its conventions. To the extent that any of us becomes profoundly individualistic and still wants to retain the name psychoanalyst, to that extent professional incoherence will develop, for the rules of the game will have been changed, and standards of understanding and practice will no longer apply across the board. Latent grandiosity mixed perhaps with some sociopathy will prevail.

My main point is that I regard my account of conformists and individualists among patients and therapists as provisional. It reflects my understanding of both contemporary ego-psychological Freudian and contemporary British Kleinian terms and practices, and I have assumed that there is enough of a community of understanding among all of us to claim, in this special sense, that I am speaking objectively. I claim to be describing reality. I assert that my account has truth value. What I don't assert is that I am describing the only possible world or, more specifically, the only possible therapeutic culture. I am prepared to accept as worthy of respect and attention other systematic presentations that are cast in other terms and use other criteria of evidence or proof—though I will not feel obliged to agree that any of them lead to a better understanding or practice.

The pluralism that I am describing does not require us to fall silent; nor does it involve an "anything goes" attitude. We go on as we have before, though with more humility about our claims about the past and the present. The reason for this is that pluralism is not a cause to be espoused or opposed. It is an aspect of every culture and subculture. Thus, all I am saying is that acknowledging this to be so in psychoanalytic therapies can be liberating and exciting and not a surrender to anal chaos.

REFERENCES

Erikson, E. (1956). The problem of ego identity. *Journal of the American Psychoanalytic Association*, 4:56–121.

Joseph, B. (1983). On understanding and not understanding: Some technical issues. *International Journal of Psycho-analysis*, 64:291–298.

Kernberg, O. (1975). *Borderline Conditions and Pathological Narcissism*. New York: Jason Aronson.

Klein, M. (1948). *Contributions to Psycho-Analysis, 1921–1945: Developments in Child and Adult Psycho-Analysis*. New York: McGraw-Hill, 1964.

Kohut, H. (1977). *The Restoration of the Self*. New York: International Universities Press.

Reich, A. (1951). On countertransference. *International Journal of Psycho-analysis*, 41:16–33.

Schafer, R. (1967). *Projective Testing and Psychoanalysis: Selected Papers*. New York: International Universities Press.

———. (1983). *The Analytic Attitude*. New York: Basic Books.

———. (1992). *Retelling a Life: Narrative and Dialogue in Psychoanalysis*. New York: Basic Books.

Steiner, J. (1993). *Psychic Retreats: Pathological Organizations in Psychotic, Neurotic, and Borderline Patients*. London and New York: Routledge.

Winnicott, D. W. (1958). *Collected Papers: Through Paediatrics to Psycho-Analysis*. New York: Basic Books.

■ 3 The Private Self and Relational Theory

Our book asks the question: what is the relation between the inner world of private meaning and the outer world of interaction? This immensely broad topic suggests the need for concepts that would bridge the gap between individual and social psychology. Psychoanalysis is preeminently a psychology of the individual, yet our field of observation is intersubjective. Traditional psychoanalysis has been defined as a one-person psychology in that it refers intersubjective events occurring within the psychoanalytic dyad to the mind of one individual, the patient. However, within the past decade there has been a noticeable shift of emphasis toward a two-person psychology. We have collectively given greater weight to the developmental significance of actual parent-child experiences as well as to the intersubjective nature of transference. This point of view has long been implicit in object relations theory and more recently has become the explicit focus of psychoanalytic studies of the infant.

Somewhat more than forty years ago, the English psychoanalyst John Rickman (1957) suggested that research in psychology be divided in accordance with the number of persons involved; hence he proposed a one-body, two-body, three-body psychology, and so forth. For example, when we consider the influence of internalized objects, Rickman noted that we can speak of a three- or four-person psychology in a two-person situation.

A recent school of psychoanalytic thought, which identifies itself as a two-person psychology, has come to be known as relational theory. I shall use this term in its more general, generic sense as a theory that rests on the premise that psychoanalysis is fundamentally intersubjective. In its more restricted sense, relational theory has been identified by some as an alternative to Freudian psychoanalysis, which, in turn, has been inaccurately described as a "drive-structure" model. My own position is to oppose such dichotomies. Even as one who does not accept Freud's instinct theory, I do not find it necessary to dichotomize relational theory and Freudian thought in this fashion; it does an injustice to the complexity and subtlety of Freud's thinking. Furthermore, Freud himself did not contrast individual and social psychologies. Freud (1921) explicitly stated in his monograph on group psychology that a psychology of the individual must perforce be, at the same time, a social psychology. Traditional structural theory can be interpreted within a social context as a theory of internalized objects; the self contains many voices. Freud posited that what was internalized as psychic structure represented a *relationship* between persons. For example, in "An Outline of Psychoanalysis" (1940), Freud described the superego's function in relation to the ego as carrying on the functions performed by people in the outside world. Freud did not further develop this line of thought; this was left to Fairbairn, who can be considered as the founder of contemporary relational theory.

Freud was as aware as we are today that the transference and countertransference are the primary sources of psychoanalytic observation. He knew that it was this unique source of observation that distinguished psychoanalysis from other psychologies. While fully aware of the intersubjective origin of the countertransference, Freud believed that to utilize the countertransference as a source of primary data would jeopardize psychoanalysis' claim to be an "objective" science. We learn this from the Freud-Ferenczi correspondence (Brabant et al., 1993). As early as the years prior to World War I, both Freud and Ferenczi knew a great deal about countertransference, but Freud advised Ferenczi not to publish papers on this subject because it might give psychoanalysis a bad reputation. He was thinking of the fact that countertransference might involve some kind of occult transfer of thoughts from the patient to the analyst and vice versa, and to reveal this connection might imperil psychoanalysis' claim to be a science. Some fifteen years earlier Freud revealed in a letter (August 7, 1901) to Fliess (Masson, 1985) that he was wounded by Fliess's assertion that Freud was a "reader of thoughts [who] merely reads his own thoughts into other people." Freud responded that if that were true it would render all his efforts valueless. So in that respect Freud was allergic to any public discussion of occult communication between analyst and analysand.

To some extent Freud was a positivist for whom a purely subjective, phenomenological account of self experiences was unscientific. Freud avoided using the term *self*; he spoke of the "I," which was rendered by Strachey into the abstract Latin term *ego*. The experiences of the self, both in isolation and in interaction with others, were referred to as a theory of psychic structures contained in a mental apparatus. But Freud did not go as far in this direction as his critics would maintain; we need to be reminded that the *I* is not equivalent to the *ego*. Further, the humanist in Freud prevented him from succumbing completely to such abstractions. Freud alternated between an anthropomorphic account of psychic structures—as if the structures themselves were persons—and a very different account in which the formation of psychic structures is seen as an impersonal process based upon the transformation of instinctual energy. Freud (1923) described the ego and the superego as if they were people, a child and its parents. As with a child and its parent, the superego is at times punitive toward the ego while at other times it is loving and protective. Interactive events occurring between the child and its caretakers were conceived as internalized events, so that the system of internalized objects could serve as representations or markers of those events. So in this sense Freud did not overlook the significance of the social environment, but rather he transposed interactional experiences into the language of an individual psyche.

This tradition has continued into our own time and is reflected in Hartmann's (1950) introduction of the concept of the self and object representations, which was further expanded through the work of Jacobson (1964) and Kernberg (1976). Elsewhere (Modell, 1984, 1993) I have been critical of the terms *self representations* and *object representations*, as they suggest an atomistic entity. Whatever these terms signify, they refer to memorialized structures without apparent links to experiences in real time.

Fairbairn (1952) greatly enlarged Freud's anthropomorphic interactional description of the ego, or more properly speaking, the self. Traumatic experiences that have occurred between the self and the caretakers become transposed into internalized object relations within the self. Fairbairn proposed that a traumatic relationship with a parent resulted in the internalization within the self of both actors, the victim and the perpetrator. If the affective experiences of both the victim and the perpetrator are internalized within the self, a relative coherence of the self cannot be maintained. Fairbairn postulated that an initially cohesive self is then split into dissociative aspects such as a central ego or self, which may or may not have conscious awareness of other aspects of the self. These split-off other aspects of the self were characterized by Fairbairn as an exciting object, a rejecting object, and a persecutory object, and so forth. In contrast to Freud, Fairbairn described the splitting of the self as a consequence of traumatic relationships. Sutherland (1989), in his biography of Fairbairn, makes the justifiable claim that Fairbairn's theory represented a Copernican revolution within psychoanalysis in that his theory of personality, unlike Freud's, was founded upon social experiences and not on the vicissitudes of individual instinctual development.

In this regard it is interesting to note that a similar criticism of Freud was made as early as 1927 by the Russian philosopher Bakhtin (1984), who noted that in a psychoanalytic session the patient's words are determined not only by the motivations of the individual but more by the interaction that comes into being in the microsociety formed by the analyst and the patient. I shall shortly return to Bakhtin's contributions to this issue.

Fairbairn's theory is essentially a theory of memorialized social relationships. Affects and speech are the missing links that would enable his theory to be applied to social interactions in real time. Fairbairn did not pay particular attention to the function of affects. In this regard Kernberg (1976) made an important contribution to the theory of internalized object relations, namely, that affects are the organizers of internalized objects. Affects are memorialized as categories of experience that form a link between past and present. In *Other Times, Other Realities* (Modell, 1990) and *The Private Self* (Modell, 1993), I have re-emphasized the importance of Freud's idea of *nachträglichkeit*, the re-contextualization of memory, suggesting that in the transference specific memories of affective experiences are recategorized.

In *The Private Self* I develop the thesis that the self is fundamentally paradoxical, which leads to certain conceptual dilemmas. Philosophers have long recognized the epistemological quandary of objectifying the subjective experience of self. Freud may have recognized this when he alternated between anthropomorphic and scientific accounts of the ego. Apart from this epistemological paradox, the self is contradictorily both private and social. The self obtains its sense of coherence and continuity from within, yet at the same time it is dependent upon the appraisal of others who can either support or disrupt the self's continuity. The private self supports a relative self-sufficiency, whereas from another perspective the self is not at all autonomous and is vulnerable in its dependence upon others for a sense of coherence and continuity.

The coherence and continuity of our private self is generated from within, and we guard against anything that intrudes upon this process. In contrast, as has been emphasized by self psychology, we also seek coherence through social affirmation. As infants we acquire human traits through the influence of others. This coherence, finding a completeness of the self in the other, is analogous, in adulthood, to the poet's use of a muse or one's use of what Kohut referred to as a mature self-object. But it should be noted again that the other who contributes to the cohesion of the self can also contribute to its disruption. The self is a homeostatic selective system aimed at maintaining its own continuity and coherence. Yet the self is at the same time an intersubjective system. As Hegel first observed, our consciousness of self is dependent upon the consciousness of the other. If we grant that the self is paradoxically both autonomous and dependent, individual and social psychology cannot be dichotomized. This paradox of the simultaneity of autonomous self-regulation and dependent intersubjectivity can be illustrated in certain well-known aspects of the transference.

For example, we know that transference is both a repeatable occurrence and a unique happening. There is some justification for the view that the transference can be used as a nosological marker, as seen in the differentiation between transference in the so-called classical neurosis with its central oedipal configuration and transference in the narcissistic disorders. We also know that when a patient has had more than one analysis, some aspects of the transference are repeated regardless of the personality, theory, and technique employed by each analyst. Yet paradoxically the transference is also a uniquely new creation that reflects the patient's response to the personality and technique of the analyst. Transference from this perspective is not repeatable inasmuch as the analyst, by virtue of his or her theoretical beliefs, will interpret some aspects of the transference and minimize or ignore other aspects.

Recognizing that both the private and social selves operate simultaneously as separate organizing foci may help us to avoid the crude pendulum shifts that have characterized conventional wisdom concerning the transference. For example, when I was a psychoanalytic candidate it was an unquestioned assumption that the analyst's contribution to the transference in a well-conducted analysis was relatively minimal, and that technique was accordingly adjusted toward this end. The analyst was viewed as a neutral screen or mirror to receive the patient's transference projections. Today there are some analysts, influenced by relational theories, who claim that the content of the transference can largely be attributed to the analyst, thereby minimizing the projective aspects of the transference and, by implication, minimizing the autonomous aspects of the private self and the patient's psychic reality.

If one needs evidence for the existence of the private self, one has only to observe the defensive measures employed to preserve it. The need to preserve the coherence and continuity of the self from intrusive disruptions is evident in most psychoanalyses. These defensive measures can be placed under the heading of the regulation of distance. As Balint (1950) noted, defenses not only are intrapsychic but also may occur between two minds. In disorders of the self, the so-called narcissistic disorders, the noncommunication of affects is one method of regulating distance. The meaning to be discovered in our speech is signaled by a certain quanta of affect. We are all familiar with those patients who fill their hours with talk that communicates nothing, so that at times we feel that we are drowning in a sea of words without meaning. Prolonged states of nonrelatedness induce a familiar countertransference response. I experience a sense of boredom and sleepy withdrawal, which has been described by others (Khan, 1986) as a state of "eerie mellow fatigue."

Winnicott's (1949) concept of the false self is another example of an interpersonal defense; a form of social compliance to prevent the private self from being known. Noncommunication of affects is not the same as a false self in that it does not represent a social compliance, but it has the same aim—that of protecting the private self from intrusion. This type of defense may become habitual in childhood in those families in which the child experiences the caretakers as excessively intrusive. What is of particular interest is that this social defense is internalized as an intrapsychic defense. *The means employed to protect private space against intrusion by others is also re-created within the self.* As a consequence, the individual loses touch with the vital affective core of the self, and life loses its zest and meaning. Some individuals becomes estranged and decentered from their own private self and are as false and inauthentic within themselves as they are with others. In the struggle to preserve private space they therefore achieve a tragic pyrrhic victory. Ironically, the fight to protect the private self continues even after the individual has lost contact with it. It is as if a householder maintained a burglar alarm long after misplacing the jewels. *In closing oneself off from others, one inadvertently closes oneself off from oneself.*

Measures to preserve the private self may appear in the cognitive as well as the affective sphere. For example, some patients need to preserve the autonomy of their own thinking by not accepting the ideas of others. We are all familiar with cases in which the patient appears to accept what we say, only to learn later that this represents a false compliance and that nothing has gotten through. These patients live within a fortress that does not permit any ideas to enter that they have not already thought of themselves. This trait is particularly evident in cases where the parent's construction of reality is unreliable, for example, if the parent is psychotic. In these cases psychic survival depends upon their inner construction of reality remaining unchallenged. I believe that these defenses against other minds that we can observe in the so-called narcissistic cases are merely an exaggeration of a process that is present in all of us.

The major point that I am attempting to make is fairly simple: there are two organizing foci within the self—one is social, that is to say, intersubjective, and the other is private and autonomous. The private and social selves develop in tandem. We know that the development of the sense of self is linked to the acquisition of language. We also know that the acquisition of language in infancy is a social act, but this does not preclude the existence of privately generated meanings that exist alongside of and parallel with language acquisition.

This view is consistent with the observations of infant and baby researchers, who have, within the past few decades, collected a vast body of empirical data about mother-child interactions. The work of Trevarthen (1989) and others has demonstrated that intersubjectivity exists at birth. Both infant and mother are able to track each other's affective responses and react to each other's affective states. The perceptual source for the infant is the mother's tone of voice and gaze—the eyes are truly the window to the soul. This interaction can be described as conversational in that there is a sense of combining the interests of two persons in an exchange of signs. But the infant is not simply a passive partner in this interaction, for, even shortly after birth, he or she is capable of self-activation and self-regulation. The mother responds to the infant's initiative in equal measure as the infant responds to the mother.

Not only does the infant seek to engage the mother, but he or she also initiates periods of disengagement. Even in infancy there is a suggestion of the infant's need for relative autonomy in that the infant, in a sense, is able to regulate his or her distance from the mother. This is done by means of an aversion of gaze, so that periods of relatedness are interspersed with periods of nonrelatedness. Lou Sander (1983) observed that by the third week of life the mother responds to the infant's needs by providing periods of relative disengagement. Intuitive mothers will provide their infants with "open space," which Sander sees as the infant's opportunity to exercise an "individually idiosyncratic and selective volitional initiative." The infant is free to follow his or her own *interests*, which may involve self-exploration or responses to low-level stimuli. Disengagement has a place of equal importance with engagement. One can infer from this the existence of an agency within the infant that is separate from the mother. Winnicott stressed the importance of the infant's first creative act, which he called the spontaneous gesture. The spontaneous gesture requires the mother's presence, but it exists independently of the mother. While language acquisition is undeniably social, I would suggest that the infant's spontaneous gesture represents an area of private meaning. This selectivity of the spontaneous gesture suggests to me the beginnings of a private self whose autonomy must be preserved.

The paradox of the autonomy of the private self and the dependency of the social self gives rise to a multiplicity of clinical dilemmas of which we are all aware. A central quandary is: How can I remain the same in the midst of the other person? How can I maintain my own voice and not be swallowed up by the other? Here we also encounter the fact that empathy is a mixed blessing. The wish to be known and understood is counterbalanced by a fear of being found and controlled. An empathic response may reinforce a fragile sense of self, or it may lead to sense of merging fusion which threatens the continuity of the self.

To maintain one's own voice in the midst of the other person means that one is free to have one's own thoughts and can select whether or not one chooses to be influenced by the other's construction of reality. The question of whose reality it is, is especially evident in cases of physical and sexual abuse of the child, where the voice of an adult may insist that nothing of significance had occurred. Ferenczi (1933) observed this problem in his famous paper "Confusion of Tongues Between Adults and the Child." The confusion of tongues refers to the child who is sexually seduced by the adult and is confused by the contradiction between his or her own language of tenderness and the adult's language of lust and hypocrisy. Ferenczi goes on to describe traumatized children's helpless anxiety, which compels them to subordinate themselves like automata to the will of the adult—to divine each of his desires and to gratify these oblivious of themselves. He makes the further telling observation that the guilt of the adult may be absorbed by the child.

We still do not really understand the process of suggestion, but it does involve a submission to the voice of the other. In the altered state of consciousness of hypnosis, the subject's powers of discrimination and judgment are suspended and replaced by the hypnotist's command. However, the concept of suggestion becomes more complicated when applied to states where the subject is fully conscious, as in psychoanalysis or psychotherapy. Freud (1920) noted that the patient's acceptance of an interpretation always depends upon some measure of suggestion. But was Freud thinking of the paradigm of the hypnotist to whom the patient passively submits? Alternatively, we can imagine that the analyst's suggestion will animate the patient and act as a fertilizing influence, enabling the patient to generate new meanings. In such cases, an initial passivity is followed by the patient's active generativity.

When new meanings are generated in an analysis, does the analyst simply facilitate the emergence of a selective process from within the patient? Alternatively, are new meanings borrowed from the analyst, bypassing the agency of the patient's self, or are new meanings arrived at conjointly? In other words, does the patient's acceptance of an interpretation represent an act of compliance or a generative process? Correspondingly, is the analyst's action one of discovery or one of invention?

Bakhtin (quoted by Wertsch, 1991) in his analysis of utterances, distinguishes speech interactions that interanimate both participants, which he characterizes as multi-voiced, in contrast to other interactions that are authoritative and univocal. As in the paradigm of hypnotic suggestion, the crucial question is whether the content of what is communicated is received passively or actively altered by the perceiver. An authoritative communication would be analogous to the transmission of a telegraph message that the receiver decodes unchanged. Authoritative discourses are fixed in their meaning, demanding a submission or allegiance. Authoritative communications are not transformed, only transmitted; new meanings are not created—they are simply passively received. Bakhtin also uses the term *ventriloquation* to refer to instances in which the speaker uses someone else's voice without investing the words with his own intention and accent. That is to say, the agency of the self is temporarily suspended. Bakhtin was referring to ordinary speech, but therapists recognize an analogous process when someone is under the sway of an unconscious identification and recreates the thoughts of the other.

A more complicated example can be seen in the phenomenon known as projective identification. I mention this term with some hesitancy as it has become bowdlerized and does not have any agreed upon definition. I would suggest that what characterizes a projective identification is an involuntary communication of affects with a specific memorial context, usually related to a chronically traumatic childhood parental interaction. The affective communication in a projective identification is involuntary as far as the patient is concerned, in that it is unconscious. For example, a patient was, as a child, subjected to unpredictable and unprovoked attacks by her father, who suffered from a wartime post-traumatic stress disorder. During an hour in which she was markedly withdrawn and depressed, she complained that I was not helping her because I was not making useful comments and interpretations. I, in turn, was feeling frustrated because I felt that in her withdrawn, mostly silent, unengaged state it was not possible to say anything meaningful. In response to her complaint, I did say that she wished me to produce something "out of the blue." I do not know why I chose that particular expression but, much to my surprise, it evoked an intense rage reaction. My experience was one of being attacked for making an innocent remark; her attack on me also felt "out of the blue." It was in fact that phrase that triggered the patient's outburst, evoking the memory of her father's attacks, which came out of the blue. The patient's affective state of the blameless victim was telegraphically communicated to me and I directly experienced it. But I also became angry in response to her attack so that the patient's experience was that I was attacking her. This was not simply a reversal of roles—we were both attacker and attacked. As Fairbairn (1952) predicted, developmental trauma results in dissociated splits within the self. In this instance the patient's attack upon me was dissociated; when we attempted to later analyze this interaction, the patient did not even recall that she was angry.

Projective identification does involve the kind of thought transfer that was of interest to Freud and Ferenczi. It is a very curious fact that what was the patient's private experience temporarily became my experience. I believe that this kind of involuntary transfer of traumatic affective memories is not limited to the process of projective identification, for the memories of trauma that parents have experienced are often unconsciously communicated to their children.

Helene Deutsch (1926) observed that aspects of the analyst's unconscious experience during an analytic hour may be traced to the analysand's occult communications. She called this process a "complementary" attitude, in contrast to empathy, which is explicit and conscious. Her observations were expanded by Racker (1968) in his contribution to the concept of projective identification. He explained Deutsch's complementary attitude as the analyst's unconscious identification with the patient's internal object. I believe that this view has been amply confirmed by clinical observation.

From Bakhtin's perspective, projective identification can be classified as an authoritative communication in that initially it is telegraphic and univocal. However, we know that there are two common outcomes of projective identifications. If a projective identification remains univocal, it can lead to a stalemating of the therapeutic process. If projective identification results in the generation of new meaning, however, it may become a decisive turning point in a psychoanalysis or psychotherapy.

It is the analyst's capacity to make use of projective identifications that determines this outcome. I have suggested in *Other Times, Other Realities* that the creation of new meaning in the therapeutic process implies a capacity to shift from one level of reality to the other. There are multiple levels of reality at play within the analytic process: ordinary life; reality that is separated off from ordinary life by the therapeutic frame; and the misidentification of the analyst, that is to say, the transference.

In partial answer to the question "How do we remain the same in the midst of the other?" I suggest that it is this capacity to experience life simultaneously at many levels of reality. This implies an acceptance of the paradox of the coexistence of merging and separateness, which may be another way of defining mental health. The acceptance of multiple levels of consciousness within the self enables us to transform a univocal communication into a dialogue. This is necessary for adaptation, for in our contemporary world human life is irreducibly multi-leveled. We are both paradoxically merged with the other and separate from the other. This represents an intrinsic dialectic, which I believe should also be reflected in our theories that conceptualize the relation between private meanings and our interaction with others.

REFERENCES

Bakhtin, M. (1984). *The Dialogical Principle*. Trans. W. Godzich. Minneapolis: University of Minnesota Press.

Balint, M. (1950). Changing therapeutic aims and techniques in psychoanalysis. *International Journal of Psycho-analysis*, 31:117–124.

Brabant, E., Falzeder, E., and Giampieri–Deutsch, P., eds. (1993). *The Cor-*

respondence of Sigmund Freud and Sándor Ferenczi. Cambridge, Mass.: Belknap/Harvard.

Deutsch, H. (1926). Occult processes occurring during psychoanalysis. In *Psychoanalysis and the Occult*, ed. G. Devereux. 1970. New York: International Universities Press, pp. 133–146.

Fairbairn, W. D. (1952). *Psychoanalytic Studies of the Personality*. London: Tavistock.

Ferenczi, S. (1933). Confusion of tongues between adults and the child. In *Final Contributions to the Problems and Methods of Psychoanalysis*. 1955. New York: Brunner/Mazel.

Freud, S. (1920). "Beyond the Pleasure Principle." *Standard Edition*, 18.

———. (1921). "Group Psychology and the Analysis of the Ego." *Standard Edition*, 18.

———. (1923). "The Ego and the Id." *Standard Edition*, 19.

———. (1940). "An Outline of Psychoanalysis." *Standard Edition*, 23.

Hartmann, H. (1950). Comments on the psychoanalytic theory of the ego. *Psychoanalytic Study of the Child*, 5:74–96.

Jacobson, E. (1964). *The Self and Object World*. New York: International Universities Press.

Kernberg, O. (1976). *Object Relations Theory and Clinical Psychoanalysis*. New York: Jason Aronson.

Khan, M. (1986). In: D. W. Winnicott, *Holding and Interpretation*. New York: Grove Press.

Masson, J., ed. and trans. (1985), *The Complete Letters of Sigmund Freud to Wilhelm Fliess*. Cambridge, Mass.: Harvard University Press.

Modell, A. (1984). *Psychoanalysis in a New Context*. New York: International Universities Press.

———. (1990). *Other Times, Other Realities*. Cambridge, Mass.: Harvard University Press.

———. (1993). *The Private Self*. Cambridge, Mass.: Harvard University Press.

Racker, H. (1968). *Transference and Countertransference*. New York: International Universities Press.

Rickman, J. (1957). *Selected Contributions to Psychoanalysis*. New York: Basic Books.

Sander, L. (1983). Polarity, paradox and the organizing process of development. In J. Call and R. Tyson, eds., *Frontiers of Infant Psychiatry*. New York: Basic Books.

Sutherland, J. (1989). *Fairbairn's Journey into the Interior.* London: Free Association Books.

Trevarthen, C. (1989). Intuitive emotions: Their changing role in communication between mother and infant. In M. Ammanitia, ed., *Affetti: Natura e sviluppo delle relazione interpersonali.* Bari: Laterza.

Wertsch, J. (1991). *Voices of the Mind.* Cambridge, Mass.: Harvard University Press.

Winnicott, D. W. 1949. Mind and its relation to the psyche-soma. In *Collected Papers.* 1958. New York: Basic Books.

C. Brooks Brenneis

■ 4 On the Relationship of Dream Content, Trauma, and Mind: A View from Inside Out or Outside In?

Dreams have long enjoyed a privileged position in psychoanalytic theory and clinical process. In recent times the "royal road" provided by dreams leads not only toward the dynamic unconscious, but also toward memories of actual traumatic events. Over and over, clinical experience appears to teach us that the past, especially a disruptive past, may be viewed, often quite literally, through a window in certain dreams. Strikingly realistic, repetitive, and anxiety provoking (Huizenga, 1990), these dreams are held to the side both clinically and conceptually, away from ordinary dreams. We call them *traumatic dreams*. Broad-reaching anecdotal clinical evidence has given this class of dreams a kind of conceptual independence which tempts therapists to think at times that we have found a transparent dream window through which a past material reality may be seen clearly.

The traumatic dream, a product of the collision of elemental forces—trauma from material reality, dreams from psychic reality—reveals in high relief the relative power and influence of the inner and outer worlds. What forms does trauma impose on dreams? Is trauma represented literally and accurately? If so, under what conditions? What forms do dreams impose on trauma? What transformations occur between trauma and dream? What resemblance to the foregoing trauma does the dream bear? An assessment of the way in which trauma affects dreams[1] and dreams affect trauma can be generated by reviewing empirical efforts to influence dream content and by examining literature reports of dreams paired with known trauma.

The concept of a traumatic dream asserts a connection between a real (known or unknown) event and the manifest content of a dream. The connection is in the nature of a *homomorphism*, that is, a similarity in outward appearance between the dream and the "event." This event leaves not only tracks, but tracks which follow a pattern homologous to the event. In conceptually setting aside such a group of dreams, we presume some very specific and potentially unique operations of the dream process. The general and ordinary process of dream formation involves subjecting internally and externally generated images to a series of transformations which are integrated and assembled to form the manifest dream. This set of transformations includes Freud's (1900) displacement, symbolization, condensation, and secondary elaboration. In a traumatic dream, images associated with a potent real event may be unaffected by this broader set of transformations or, more precisely in line with my definition, may be affected only by a restricted set of limited, literal transformations which preserve the original, or a clearly homologous form, of the material stimuli.

1. The impact of trauma on formal dream properties has been much studied. Brenneis (1994) reviewed this literature and concluded that no formal dream properties were exclusive to dreams based on trauma.

THE ISOMORPHIC TRAUMATIC DREAM

In principle there exists a special case in which the trauma and the dream are isomorphic, or absolutely identical. This unique psychic phenomenon deserves a close look.

The above depiction of the dream process as the interpolation of a set of transformations between some form of initial images or experiences and the dream product grossly simplifies matters. There is seldom such a thing—in any isolated or objective form—as an initial image. Beyond this, one must also include the level of arousal or stress which exists in an individual throughout the period of dream production. The period of dream production (rather than a REM interval) is referred to because the processes which are integral to the final production of a dream must include wide-ranging perceptions and memory storage which long predate the actual interval of dreaming. Recall of such stored material as well as the final fashioning of the dream and the verbal communication of the dream to a second party are also subprocesses in the formation of what is called, finally, a dream.

We have enumerated perception, memory, recall, fashioning, and communication as phases in the production of a dream. Each of these junctures, or complex subphases, are open to the interpolation of transformations. The concept of an isomorphic traumatic dream asserts that such "complexly motivated psychic products" (Renik, 1981, p. 177) may be generated which *completely* bypass transformative processes to yield a faithful reproduction of the traumatic event. These transformative processes must be bypassed at *every* phase or juncture of dream production—perception, memory storage and retrieval, fashioning, and communication. In addition, this must be accomplished under conditions of extreme stress or arousal, circumstances we believe increase rather than diminish the impact of such personal transformations. In short, the existence of an isomorphic dream requires camera-like objectivity at every processing phase from an individual in a state of extreme distress and peril.

Whatever weight is carried by these considerations could be lessened by the presentation of a counterexample. Can we find an isomorphic trauma and manifest dream pairing? A careful review of the literature leads to a surprising conclusion: statements of equivalence are made by researchers and clinicians, but actual dream texts are almost never presented. Bonaparte (1947), Renik (1981), van der Kolk et al. (1984), and Terr (1979, 1990) make explicit reference to dreams which are "exact replicas" (van der Kolk et al., 1984) of a trauma, or "accurately [repeat them] in faithful detail" (Renik, 1981). The only quoted texts are to be found in Terr's (1979) study of children abducted and buried for hours in a dimly lit truck trailer at Chowchilla, California. One (of two cited) "exact repeat playback dreams" (p. 589) reads in its entirety: "I dream when the man gets on—when we get on the vans." Impressively, van der Kolk et al. based their "exact replica" conclusion on the dreamers' statements of equivalence without collecting *any* accounts of dreams (Hartmann, personal communication, 1993).

In addition, there is no research evidence that discrete images or experiences may be literally transposed into manifest dream content. As reported by Freud (1900), Maury applied a variety of stimuli (tickling with a feather, smelling cologne, pinching lightly, etc.) to a sleeping subject. While each of the stimuli seems to have had a discernable impact on the ensuing dream, the form of that impact was never identical to the stimulus.

In contrast to this informal research, the same question has been pursued more carefully by Fisher and Paul (1959). Subjects were presented subliminally with either a double profile or clock image, following which their dreams during REM sleep were recorded. Experienced dream researchers serving as judges were given a pair of dreams—one from each stimulus—and asked to assign each member of the pair to a pre-dream stimulus. Seven of ten judges performed at better than chance, suggesting that something about the pre-dream stimulus was visible in the manifest content. The test is weakened, however, by three factors: the paired assignment design, the judges' prior knowledge of the experimental stimuli, and the tepid quality of the pre-dream stimuli.

Witkin and Lewis (1965) offer a much more elaborate and scrupulously constructed experiment that permits us to explore carefully the question of whether highly charged pre-sleep stimuli find expression in subsequent dreams, and, more informally, whether the pre-sleep stimuli can be derived from the dreams. Subjects were shown movies with explicit and charged bodily and sexual implications, and then they reported dreams from later REM awakenings.

Let us approach the latter question first by providing some of the dream imagery without indicating its likely source: (1) a troop-carrier plane with parachutists jumping out of it; (2) a hot closet; and (3) white gloves on a girl's arms (pp. 829–830). These images were culled by the authors from many dream reports as among the most vivid and clear-cut representations of aspects of a pre-sleep film. It is *not* obvious, unless one knows the film, that all refer to a vivid birth scene. The authors suggest that the troop carrier is derived from the pregnant woman, the closet from the vagina, and the white gloves from the obstetrician's bloody gloves.

There is no doubt that film images find expression in the dreams, but it is impressive that there are *no* literal transpositions of any of the pre-sleep films into the manifest dreams. Witkin and Lewis conclude that "the identification of an element in a dream as related to a pre-sleep stimulus relies on the intuitive interpretation of a symbolic or metaphoric dream translation" (p. 829). The body is replaced by "congruently structured and functioning mechanical objects" (p. 835). These transformations are highly personal and often focus on peripheral details, or central details which omit significant portions of the films' latent meanings. Not only can we not divine the film from the dream alone, but also , having seen the films, we could not predict the dream images, which are apparent only once one knows the film.

In an even more dramatic study, DeKoninck and Koulack (1975) showed subjects a film about industrial accidents in which a worker is impaled by a board and dies. Even this level of intense stimulation did not result in a single exact reproduction of a film element in any dream from any subject.

Nonetheless, some clinical evidence indicates that, under specific conditions, literal dream incorporation of traumatic experience occasionally occurs (Bonaparte, 1947; Rapaport, 1968; Wilmer, 1982, 1986; Lisman-Pieczanski, 1990; Chasseguet-Smirgel, 1992; Siegel, 1992).

The Lion Hunter's dreams are a classical example (Bonaparte, 1947). A professional ranger and hunter named W is on horseback when lion A approaches him from the front and attacks. W manages to evade this lion, only to be snatched by a second lion, B. B grabs him by his shoulder and drags him off to the base of a tree. W unsheathes his knife and strikes B three times, wounding the lion and causing it to retreat. W climbs the tree and, to avoid falling, straps himself to the tree. Lion A returns and prowls around the tree. W's party hears his cries and finds him. Three days later, after much travail, W is attended by a physician and miraculously recovers.

One of the dreams reported by W, as best as can be determined by Bonaparte the dream most proximal to the trauma, is as follows: "I am out hunting lions, find a troop of them and fire at and hit one and it at once charges me. I fire again but the shot does not go off. I run to a tree close by, climb up it, and get out of reach of the lion whereupon a very big bull buffalo appears and starts butting the tree with his head. The tree sways to and fro and I fall. Then I waken to find it is only a dream for which I am terribly thankful" (p. 5).

This dream retains the core of the trauma—W is confronted by a lion and escapes to a tree from which he fears being dislodged—but is nonetheless remarkably altered. The knife becomes a gun, and the initial close encounter, a remote one. Lion A reappears as a bull buffalo who butts rather than prowls around the tree. Finally, in the trauma B attacks W and then W attacks B, whereas in the dream, this action sequence is reversed.

For a second example, a woman who lost her home in the 1991 Oakland fires dreamt that she was "suddenly watching a woman burn alive in a building. I was watching her. There was nothing I or anyone else could do. She was terrified as she clutched the front of the charred building— flames all around her" (Siegel, 1992, p. 5). The fire and its destructive implications for this helpless woman are literally portrayed. However, even here a substitution has been made: it is not her house that burns in the dream but another building and another woman. Significantly, when she was a child this woman's family home had been destroyed by fire.

In a similar fashion, Rappaport (1968) dreams about his concentration camp experience, and combat soldiers, about combat (Wilmer, 1982, 1986). In all of these situations, the dreamer was cognitively prepared for the trauma (because it was in the line of duty, had happened before, or was repeated), traumatized as an adult, and had access to memory of the trauma. As may be gauged by the Lion Hunter's dreams, no observer could identify which dream elements were relatively untransformed without knowledge of the trauma.

In sum, there is no empirical evidence and only limited clinical evidence to support *any* isomorphic transposition of traumatic experience into dream content, except under the restricted conditions noted above. Even then, dream transformations are so encompassing that it is impossible, without knowing the trauma, to identify which dream components are isomorphic.

Freud's conclusion about Maury's experiments is equally applicable to the clinical and research evidence I have reviewed: "We may have a suspicion that the sensory stimuli which impinges on the sleeper plays only a modest part in generating his dreams and that other factors determine the choice of the mnemic images which are aroused in him" (1900, p. 29). Material reality is nearly always transformed. In those rare instances when it appears relatively untransformed, the dreamer's mind has been specifically prepared for the trauma.

THE HOMOMORPHIC TRAUMATIC DREAM

When we examine dream texts which can be paired with trauma texts, it becomes apparent that the relationship between them is homomorphic, not isomorphic.[2] A range of examples will make this clear.

2. See also Grinker and Spiegel (1945) and Kanzer (1949) for dream responses to war trauma; Levitan (1965), to shocking news; Horowitz (1986, pp. 217–226), to witnessing a suicide; Terr (1985), to a friend's rape and murder; Terr (1990), to accidental injury.

Rappaport (1968) reports the following dream from a middle-aged Polish concentration camp survivor: "She and hundreds of other women were pulled high up in an open elevator and then all blood and fat was sucked out of the women and pumped through pipes into a big kettle" (p. 716). The dream leaves no doubt that the dreamer sees herself as an indistinguishable unit in the Nazis' bestial, inhuman rendering of fat.

An Israeli colonel, who as a child during World War II wandered through central Europe on his own, dreams recurrently that "I am on a conveyor belt moving relentlessly toward a metal compactor. Nothing I can do will stop that conveyor belt and I will be carried to my end, crushed to death" (Felman and Laub, 1992, p. 79). There is no mistaking this man's view of his helpless position against the Nazis' relentless, crushing power.

Rappaport, also a concentration camp survivor, after discussing many of his own dreams makes this observation: "I never dream about specific traumatic experiences in the camp such as . . . [recounts specific memory]" (p. 729).

These dreams resonate with instances of massive and repeated trauma. It is impossible to track the precise transformations which lead to the metaphoric renditions presented in the dreams. Circumscribed traumatic events permit this. Accompanied by his wife and others, Loewenstein's (1949) patient suffered a violent canoe accident in which he was separated from the others and swept away by a torrential current. Clinging desperately to his canoe for miles, he barely managed to hang on while he was pulled underwater through powerful rapids. He emerged "helpless and exhausted" near the rest of his party and was carried to shore.

Loewenstein writes that the night after the accident the patient had the following dream: "He is shut in the highest room of a tower. An elderly woman is trying to prevent him from escaping. He succeeds in diving through the floors, ceilings, and walls of the different rooms of the tower, one after the other. He arrives below in a yard, shut off by a large porte-cochère. He hesitates to ring for the concierge and dives through the door, turning outside to the right with a feeling of enormous relief" (pp. 449–450). The patient's dream *on the night of the accident* has so fully transformed the trauma that it is highly unlikely the trauma can be deciphered from the dream. Yet it so aptly conveys the trauma that once it is described, the homomorphism between trauma and dream is immediately obvious. The traumatic event has been simultaneously rendered and transformed beyond recognition into an almost mythic and fanciful escape.

A significant number of the dreams Terr (1979) reports from the abducted Chowchilla children have this same quality: an expressively apt metaphor which simultaneously personalizes and conceals the details of the original traumatic experience. Examples include: "I had a dream in a castle. I was a princess with a big giant catching me, grabbing me. He grabbed me by the shirt and ripped it off." "Someone will get me and take me away in the ocean. You'd go down and down with the fish. The shark would eat me" (pp. 589–590).

A final example is provided by the dream of an evacuee of the 1991 Oakland firestorm (Siegel, 1992). A man whose home was unexpectedly saved from destruction by an air-dropped fire retardant reported this dream: "In my house watching the flood waters rise. Soon I look out the window and the ocean waters are coming right up to the edge of the house . . . water starts leaking in. . . . Then as I watch out the window, the flood recedes like in the movie *The Ten Commandments*" (p. 6).

In all of these examples, no element from the preceding trauma is literally transposed into the manifest content. Heinous Nazi crimes become large-scale fat rendering, and their relentless power, an unstoppable conveyor belt moving toward a metal compactor. Being trapped in an engulfing river is depicted as being held captive by an elderly woman in a tower. A big giant replaces kidnappers, while the buried truck trailer is replaced by being down in the ocean with the fish. Receding waters reminiscent of biblical stories represent miraculously delivered fire retardant. At the same time that each element is transformed, the experience of the trauma is reassembled in such a way as to provide a highly personalized recapitulation of the experience.

ANALYSIS

If we represent an element of the original trauma by s and its corresponding dream component as s', we can trace out some implications from the above summary of traumatic dream transformations. First, the data do not offer much support for a literal transposition of s into s' where (s=s'). A significant amount of clinical and experimental evidence suggests that the process is of turning s into s', where s' represents a transformation of s. For example, the Lion Hunter's knife becomes a gun.

This formulation, however, is clearly incomplete, for our evidence indicates that an invisible middle step occurs in all transformations. The Lion Hunter's knife registers as a member of a class of objects which have some functional or structural similarity; that is, a class of homomorphic elements. If we call this class G, then it is apparent that s first maps into G, from which some other element may be withdrawn to yield s'. Thus, although s and s' belong to G, s' cannot be derived independently by an observer from G, nor can s be predicted from s', for they are only two of a multitude of homomorphic elements in G. Examples from the data abound: Loewenstein's canoeist represents two distinct aspects of the river in separate images—the river's gravity-driven dimension as a tower, and its grasping quality as an elderly woman who holds him captive. For the Israeli officer, crushing power is represented as a metal compactor. Between the trauma and the dream representation must be an abstract class G of homomorphic elements.

The transformative process becomes even more complex when we add a reverse transformation. This interposes yet another step between s and s', for G, as a class, is replaced by "the opposite of G." Now we have the situation reflected, for example, in the transformation of naked bodies into elaborately clothed dream figures or bloody gloves into white gloves from Witkin's study. The Lion Hunter's close encounter becomes one at a distance. Siegel (1992) reports a number of dreams of growth, flowering, and pregnancy from the firestorm survivors.

Further still, if we include metonymy among our transformations, an incidental aspect of s may become the basis for the transformation.

Metonymy appears in the dreamer's focus on a single element to represent a much more complex experience. Such an instance is a repetition of a dream image of "using hands" after viewing the obstetric film (Witkin and Lewis, 1965, p. 830).

Most of the transformations employed—symbolization, displacement, condensation—make use of the *substitution of functionally equivalent forms*. Beyond this, however, the process is made much more complex by transformations of reversal and metonymy. As was demonstrated above, these transformations may result in highly skewed or distorted dream representations of trauma.

To return to our analysis, if elements s and s′ are psychically equivalent, one may wonder why a replacement item s′ comes into play at all? In most cases the dreamer does not thereby minimize or attenuate his risk or peril in the traumatic dreams we have reviewed. Descriptively, what happens fits most closely with Piaget's (1968) concept of assimilation, by which perceptions are fitted into pre-existing mental schema. Traumatic experiences, as they are represented in dreams, then, reflect an almost instantaneous assimilation. We may surmise, however, that compromise formation as much as cognitive familiarity is involved. Several examples from above will be instructive. The abducted child who dreams of herself as a princess grabbed by a giant has probably assimilated the experience into a pre-existing oedipal fantasy. The canoeist assimilates his capture by the river into a fantasy of trying to escape from an elderly woman, a fantasy which Loewenstein tells us has highly personal meanings for the dreamer. The Lion Hunter renders his knife as a gun, perhaps reflecting both his greater professional reliance on a gun, but also his wish for a more potent weapon which allows for strength to be wielded at a distance. Thus, *pre-existing* adaptive cognitive schema, fantasies, or compromise formations—all varieties of assimilation—may be called into play in the transformation of any given image.

The notion of assimilation illuminates the most striking example we have of a traumatic dream which most directly reveals its origins, namely, the Lion Hunter's dreams. One might argue that W's dreams are transformed, but because the risk of a lion's attack would be a daily professional possibility, the fantasy (or cognitive appreciation) of exactly such an occurrence precedes the attack. This would allow for what appears to be some literal transposition of the trauma into the dream: the category of experience to be assimilated already exists. A similar case might be made, for example, if a steeplejack fell or a policeman were shot and each dreamed directly about that. This idea is borne out in the firestorm survivor's dream of the woman burning alive, for this woman's childhood home had burned down. Destruction by fire was a pre-existing category with great weight.

Even though we can enumerate and describe the types of transformations interposed between specific experience and certain manifest dreams, we cannot predict what specific content may be subject to transformation by substitution or by reversal. We cannot even say what kind of content is most likely to be subjected to a particular type of transformation. Similarly, it is impossible at present to infer from any given dream content what type of transformation has been applied during the process of dreaming.

If we stop our analysis here, however, we miss the most significant observation: Whatever dream transformations are performed on the specifics of a traumatic experience, the resultant dream is an emotionally accurate metaphoric depiction of the experience as much as it is a distortion of specific experience. Individual transformations are subordinated to an overriding synthetic aim—to represent the experience in an affectively apt fashion. A dynamic emotional drama remains relatively invariant. For example, the Lion Hunter's dream portrays the idea "kill or be killed"; the Israeli colonel's, "I am doomed"; the man whose house is spared, "only a miracle will save us"; and the canoeist, "I am trapped and must escape." While this paradigm appears to be generally true, on occasion that higher-order representational aim produces an inverted dream. In these instances the trauma is reversed: destructive fire becomes fresh growth (Siegel, 1992), and naked bodies are elaborately clothed (Witkin and Lewis, 1965).

Whichever form this pattern takes—direct or reverse—it is clear that these dream renditions are more poignant and evocative than literal replays of the traumas themselves. One might conclude that apt personal representation, not attenuation of the trauma, is the overriding feature of these dreams. Apt representation in itself, then, must reflect the highest form of attenuation and mastery: "I have taken this traumatic event and made it truly and uniquely my own." While the trauma dictates the terms of the event, as it were, the subject, in his or her dreams, dictates the forms in which the event is ultimately structured.

DISCUSSION

As we have seen with dreams and trauma, in shaping personal experience even the most massive events interact with a decisive partner, the mind. There is no such thing as an exact replica in the mind of even the most potent event. Even with cognitive preparation, there are no unmediated experiences. We can no more strip away our implicit biases than we can strip away our skeletal structure. The core of our experience is unavoidably and necessarily subjectively interpreted: each mind has a life of its own. But what does it mean to say that the mind has a life of its own? What does the phrase "apt personal representation" mean? Or the earlier phrase "higher-order aim?" Higher than what?

To pursue these questions, let us examine the transformations the canoeist's mind interposes between his accident and his dream. For example, although the force of gravity remains a constant, the horizontal dimension of the river becomes a vertical axis in the tower. The swollen river which held him captive is personified as an elderly woman trying to keep him from escaping. The event shifts from being helplessly swept away to diving intentionally from room to room and floor to floor: the passive mode becomes active. Finally, the treacherous enclosing rapids seem to be rendered as the enclosed yard opened only by a porte-cochère. Affect is unchanged: relief is clearly portrayed and desperation implied in the dream.

Some of these transformations convey a simple equivalence: the bodily experience of being pulled downstream in the river is reoriented to become diving down from a height. A similar direct parallel may seem to exist between the engulfing river and the enclosed yard with only a narrow opening as an escape. The directness of this transformation may be deceptive, however, for this imagery conveys not only a measure of geometric congruence, but also the dangers of psychological entrapment. The personification of the river as an elderly woman reinforces this idea: women, like water, may entrap and leave one desperate to escape. And the dream escape, in contrast to the real-life experience, occurs through decisive, purposeful actions.

Clearly, the dream has assimilated (Piaget, 1968) the desperate experience in the river to some pre-existing mental schema. The structure of even simple transformative assimilations reflect complex cognitive operations. Powerful abstracting capabilities are needed to appreciate that the kinesthetic sensation of being pulled downstream is a sensorimotor equivalent to the sensation of falling downward. The mind, without conscious effort, abstracts this central parallel and selects a more familiar form for the internal representation of this bodily experience. Even more impressively complex is the transformation between the river and the elderly woman. In this instance a kinesthetic experience has been matched with an experience from an entirely different realm: the physically engulfing river becomes the physically and psychologically entrapping elderly woman. Additionally, by transforming a passive mode into an active one, initiative displaces helplessness and creates an adaptive opportunity where none existed.

What is most remarkable is that, however the particulars have been transformed, an essential gestalt has been not only retained but enhanced with personal meaning. The dreamer's kinesthetic experience remains unchanged—struggling against gravity; his goal is escape; his emotional state is life-and-death desperation. Yet even so, an impersonal event has been assimilated, piece by piece, into a vivid dream in highly personal terms. The dream has simultaneously transformed the trauma beyond recognition, beautifully preserved it in mythic, fanciful forms, and created a purposeful escape. The whole exceeds the sum of its parts. Like an artistic creation, it succeeds far beyond the mechanisms of any delineated set of transformations. As significant as those transformations may be, the product, in its ultimate shape, is determined by some higher-order aim.

Transformed pieces like the above are arranged not willy-nilly, but rather in a manner and form which is both creative and conservative: new experiences shaped by old forms to make something both old and familiar and new and unique. Basically, these higher-order psychic processes are large-scale organizing templates. This may be illustrated by analogy. Subatomic particles, elemental though they be, exist in isolation only under the most extraordinary circumstances. They tend overwhelmingly to collect, not haphazardly, but in recurrent patterns. They seek affinities, sometimes with like, sometimes with unlike. More complex structures build up, not randomly, but rather because some pieces fit. These ordered collections tend to stay together; the ordering lends stability. These ordered collections also tend to exert and seek affinities of their own.

While entropy, or decay into randomness, may be a fundamental property of physical systems, its opposite, a move toward ordered forms, must be an equally fundamental property. Elements move toward more complexly ordered forms or coherencies because they are actually simplifications. An ordered collection contains more information because the structure itself codes information.

These same ideas about physical systems also apply to psychical systems. The mind optimizes mental activity by structuring psychic experience in such a way that the most information can be placed in the least space. Increasingly complex ordering, which subsumes content under structure, may be the way the mind accomplishes this.

The forms these organizing templates take are inclusive, varied, and yet precisely personal. As we have seen, they range from sensorimotor equivalence (canoeist), functional equivalence (viewers of obstetric film), cognitive familiarity (Lion Hunter), and psychodynamically structured fantasies (canoeist and Chowchilla children), to adaptive opportunities (Lion Hunter, canoeist). They pull raw psychic material into their orbit of influence, generating an amalgam of old orderings suffused with new material. They simultaneously conserve and create, and wed process to form.

One might somewhat fancifully describe these organizing forces as a kind of marvelous psychic topology. In mathematics, topology examines structural properties which are retained through particular deformations. Structures are called homomorphic (in topology, homeomorphic) if one can be turned into the other by certain transformations. It appears as if the mind functions topologically; that is, transforms immediate experience into pre-existing topologically homomorphic structures. These homomorphic structures are the overarching forces in psychic life. They exert force, not from the bottom up, so to speak, but from the top down. Complex, highly ordered, and stable, they compress the building blocks of immediate experience into precisely coded personal statements which constitute the heart of who we are psychologically. Events are topologically transformed into a network of compact cognitive and affective allusion which preserves fundamental aspects of outer experience in precise personal terms.

From this vantage point, we are positioned squarely in the midst of what Sperry (1993) terms the "cognitive revolution." Lower-order (biochemical) mechanisms interact causally in a "reciprocal up-down paradigm" (p. 882) with higher-order (psychical) mechanisms. Neither is dominant, nor can one be reduced to the other: psychology forms biology as much as biology forms psychology. Sperry's "higher-level (yet-to-be-described) cognitive system of cerebral processing" (p. 882) has been described above, in a broad and preliminary fashion, as a system of psychic topology. "No longer written off as ineffectual epiphenomena nor reduced to microphenomena," this personal topology, in our terms, "becomes the most critically powerful force shaping today's civilized world" (p. 879). In potent measure, the outer world *is* what the inner world makes of it.

I began this chapter with the notion that the traumatic dream might provide a view from the inside out; that is, a view of material reality seen through a relatively transparent psychic window. I end with exactly the opposite impression. The most revealing perspective is from the outside in; that is, a view of the magnificent capacity of the human mind to create information-dense, stable, coherent templates of subjective meaning: the mind their architect and builder.

This chapter was awarded the first Austen Riggs Center–Rapaport-Klein Study Group Scientific Prize in 1994.

REFERENCES

Bonaparte, M. (1947). A lion hunter's dreams. *Psychoanalytic Quarterly*, 16:1–10.
Brenneis, B. (1994). Can early trauma be reconstructed from dreams? On the relationship of dreams to trauma. *Psychoanalytic Psychology*, 11:429–447.
Chasseguet-Smirgel, J. (1992). Some thoughts on the psychoanalytic situation. *Journal of the American Psychoanalytic Association*, 40:3–25.
DeKoninck, J., and Koulack, D. (1975). Dream content and adaptation to a stressful situation. *Journal of Abnormal Psychology*, 84:250–260.
Felman, S., and Laub, D. (1992). *Testimony*. New York: Routledge.
Fisher, C., and Paul, I. (1959). The effect of subliminal visual stimulation on images and dreams. *Journal of the American Psychoanalytic Association*, 7:35–83.
Freud, S. (1900). *The Interpretation of Dreams. Standard Edition*, 4 and 5.
Grinker, R., and Spiegel, J. (1945). *Men Under Stress*. Philadelphia: Blakiston.
Horowitz, M. (1986). *Stress Response Syndromes*, 2nd ed. New York: Jason Aronson.
Huizenga, J. (1990). Incest as trauma: A psychoanalytic case. In H. Levine, ed., *Adult Analysis and Childhood Sexual Abuse*, pp. 117–135. Hillside, N.J.: Analytic Press.
Kanzer, M. (1949). Repetitive nightmares after a battlefield killing. *Psychiatric Quarterly Supplement*, 23:120–126.
Levitan, H. (1965). A traumatic dream. *Psychoanalytic Quarterly*, 34:265–267.
Lisman-Pieczanski, N. (1990). Counter-transference in the analysis of an adult who was sexually abused as a child. In H. Levine, ed., *Adult Analysis and Childhood Sexual Abuse*, pp. 137–147. Hillside, N.J.: Analytic Press.
Loewenstein, R. (1949). A post-traumatic dream. *Psychoanalytic Quarterly*, 18:449–454.

Piaget, J. (1968). *Six psychological studies*. New York: Vintage Books.

Rappaport, E. (1968). Beyond traumatic neurosis. *International Journal of Psycho-analysis*, 49:719–731.

Renik, O. (1981). Typical dreams, "super-ego dreams," and traumatic dreams. *Psychoanalytic Quarterly*, 50:159–189.

Siegel, A. (1992). Dreaming patterns of firestorm victims. Presentation, Association for the Study of Dreams, Santa Cruz, Calif., June 24, 1992.

Sperry, R. (1993). The impact and promise of the cognitive revolution. *American Psychologist*, 48:878–885.

Terr, L. (1979). Children of Chowchilla: A study of psychic trauma. *Psychoanalytic Study of the Child*, 34:547–623.

———. (1985). Remembered images and trauma. *Psychoanalytic Study of the Child*, 40:483-533.

———. (1990). *Too Scared to Cry*. New York: Harper and Row.

van der Kolk, B., Briz, R., Burr, W., Sherry, S., and Hartmann, E. (1984). Nightmares and trauma: A comparison of nightmares after combat with lifelong nightmares in veterans. *American Journal of Psychiatry*, 141:187–190.

Wilmer, H. (1982). Vietnam and madness: Dreams of schizophrenic veterans. *Journal of the American Academy of Psychoanalysis*, 10:47–65.

———. (1986). Combat nightmares: Toward a theory of violence. *Spring*, 46:120–139.

Witkin, H., and Lewis, H. (1965). The relation of experimentally induced pre-sleep experiences to dreams. *Journal of the American Psychoanalytic Association*, 13:819–849.

Joyce McDougall

If the soul within is more real
than the outer world, as you,
philosopher, pretend
Why then is it the outer world
that is offered to me as the
model of reality?
—Fernando Pessoa

◼ 5 The Artist and the Outer World

For many years I have been attempting to capture a glimpse into the mysterious origins of creative expression, through exploring the impact upon myself of certain creative works, as well as studying the creative process and its inhibitions in my analysands. Whether the medium be writing, painting, sculpture, music, the performing arts, scientific and intellectual creativity, or innovation in the worlds of politics, business, or industrial invention, there is an enigmatic dimension to creative activity that evades our comprehension.

Freud himself searched constantly for the secrets of creativity. In his essay on creative writers and day dreaming (1908), he asks: "From what sources does that strange being [the creative writer] draw his material?" He replies that a creative writer behaves like a child at play in that he creates a world of his own. Freud states that "(the child) creates a world of phantasy which he takes very seriously . . . (and) invests with large amounts of emotion." However, Freud goes on to say, "as people grow up they cease to play (and furthermore the adult) knows that he is expected not to go on playing or phantasying any longer." Later in the same essay he proclaims, "we may lay it down that a happy person never phantasies, only an unsatisfied one." This somewhat critical attitude to fantasy life in adulthood appears throughout Freud's writings, as though fantasies—and even the enjoyment of contemplating creative works— were a guilty preoccupation.

The analytic world had to wait for D. W. Winnicott to convey a more optimistic view of fantasy, play, and creativity. Winnicott's designation of the "intermediate area of experiencing," in which both the inner world and the outer world participate, is a fertile concept for probing the perplexities of the creative process—as well as elucidating the question of creative and intellectual inhibitions. As Winnicott (1971) defines it: "(the area of transitional space) widens out into that of play, of artistic creativity and appreciation, of religious feeling and of dreaming." Although both Freud and Winnicott advance the notion that the creative individual is playing, this must not be taken to mean that creative activity is carefree. On the contrary, creative and innovative activity is linked with considerable violence and frequently arouses intense experiences of anguish and guilt. The resistance to allowing oneself to work is a common experience to the creative artist, and my analysands have shown me that this is most acutely experienced when they feel particularly inspired by a pristine vision, invention, or idea that is clamoring for expression.

It was not until Melanie Klein (1945) began considering art as a reflection of the earliest relations between infant and mother that new light was thrown upon the inner world of the creative being. She emphasized, perhaps more clearly than any other psychoanalytic writer, the dimension of violent emotion in the primal substratum of the human psyche. This concept has interested me because years of observation and reflection have led me to perceive that violence is an essential element in creative production. Apart from the force and intensity of the creative urge in itself, innovators are violent beings to the extent that they exercise their power to impose on the external world their thoughts, their images, their dreams or their nightmares.

It is not incomprehensible that a quota of anxiety and psychic conflict so often accompanies the act of creating, but we must also remember that creative people tend to seek psychoanalytic help at times when their productivity is endangered or even paralyzed. Thus we are presented with a privileged insight into not only the factors that contribute to creative activity but also those that lie behind the sudden failure to create.

However, before taking into consideration the symptoms and inhibitions that are liable to arise when conflicts in the inner universe of creative individuals are projected onto the outer world, I should like to comment on the popular myth of the creator as unsuccessful and having a reputation for emotional instability and perverse or psychotic potentialities. In fact, the lives of many famous creators are as varied in history and psychological structure as are those of the average banker, butcher, plumber, or politician. Many of them have led rather ordinary bourgeois existences. Some have been devoted parents. Others have combined their creative work with successful activities in other fields. Rubens was named ambassador, Matisse began his professional life as a lawyer, Chekhov was a doctor, Claudel was a diplomat, Mussorgsky was a lieutenant, to mention only a few.

It is also worthy of note that the majority of creative artists, in whatever field, are astonishingly productive. It took years to catalogue Mozart's compositions. Rubens painted thousands of pictures. By the age of sixteen Toulouse-Lautrec had completed fifty paintings and three hundred drawings. Van Gogh's production, even during his most serious psychological illness, would fill a small museum. Euripides wrote ninety-two plays. Donizetti composed sixty-three operas. Thomas Edison patented more than a thousand inventions.

With regard to those creators who have manifested psychotic, perverse, or psychopathic behavior, the part of the personality which allowed them to create, and to keep on creating, must be considered as the *healthy* part! We might envisage the internal universe of the creative individual as something like a volcano. The live volcano conceals within its depths continual heat and churning energy and will send out sparks, rocks, and flames at appropriate moments, but a prolonged blockage would precipitate an explosion.

One of my analysands, who became a renowned painter, wrote the following lines to me in a long letter, after the end of her analysis, summing up what she had learned:

> The profound primordial drives that surge up in me can become powerful enough to cause discomfort; the constant build up of tension has to be put outside me into the outer world in order to restore some feeling of harmony inside. It is creation but it is fired by feelings of destruction. When I cannot paint I become the target of my own violent aggression.
>
> I understand so well the frustration of my dear friend [A] who says he hates his paintings because "they never depict the painting I have in my mind." Then there is [B] who every so often destroys every painting he still has in his studio. Is this what Freud called the "death instinct"?

It is possible that the drive to self-destructiveness is always in action during any creative process and, once the work is set in motion, becomes part of the movement that brings fragmentation and structure together. This recalls Modell's concept of the two selves (chapter 3).

Patients often encounter feelings of depression, self-hatred, anger, and frustration, leading to a wish to destroy the work in progress. At this point such patients may resemble the persons with personality disorders described by Shapiro in chapter 1. Here the outer world may play a beneficial role or, on the contrary, reflect back to the creator everything that he or she most fears. Creative personalities in psychotherapy or analysis rarely present as the neurotic patients whom Shapiro suggests have a stable psychic structure—an inner frame, so to speak—whereas artists (in all fields) are more likely to "crash against boundaries," as Shapiro puts it. They then tend toward the externalization he describes, in which "the third" becomes the public that receives the full force of the projective identification that is at work. Here I find enlightening Shapiro's concept of utilizing the "external managerial frame" (which the public becomes, in a sense, for the innovator and creator), in that public rejection or other hard realities that come to the fore can be used to interpret the extent to which this "third" is an unconscious repetition of familiar family patterns of the past.

ASPECTS OF THE CREATIVE ACT

Before dealing with certain fundamental aspects of the creative process observed in clinical work, I should like to emphasize that psychoanalysis does not claim to hold the key to explicating artistic creativity; on the contrary, therapists hope that artists and their created works will draw us closer to *discovering* the key to human nature.

Clinical considerations have led me to the overall impression that creativity, while its specifics will always elude us, springs originally from the erogenic body and the way in which its drives are represented and its somatic functions structured by the caretakers of infancy. In attempting to follow the complex links among the creator, the created work, and the public, four fundamental aspects seem to form part of the background to any creative thought or act. Two of these concern the creator's relation to the *external world*, namely (1) the struggle with the medium of expression and (2) the nature of the individual's relationship to the imagined public for whom the created product is intended. The other two factors pertain to the *internal world*, namely (3) the role of pregenital sexuality (including oral, anal, and phallic drives) and (4) the importance of the unconscious bisexual wishes of infancy and the nature of their integration into the psychic structure.

My analysands have taught me that each of these four factors may be experienced as a form of *transgression*, and are likely, therefore, to arouse psychic conflict and inhibit productivity. Production may continue, but at tremendous cost in terms of panic anxiety, profound depression, or other forms of psychic suffering. Schafer's description (chapter 2) of the "secret transgressors" who are terrorized by the thought of being discovered is intriguing in this regard. In many ways artistic personalities also frequently deal with "fragmented selves and objects" and seek a sense of individuality and cohesion through their created works or inventions. At the same time they display themselves as "conspicuous individualists" in Schafer's sense.

Let us look first at the artist in relation to the outer world before considering transactions in the world of psychic reality.

THE EXTERNAL WORLD

The Creator and the Medium

Underlying the struggle of every creative person with his or her chosen medium of expression is always a fantasy of fusion, or confusion, with the medium itself. This gives rise to contradictory feelings; the creator wishes at the same time to caress the medium of expression and to attack it in the effort to master it. Such conflicts are clearly observable among painters and sculptors, who will often destroy the work they are trying to create. Musicians frequently complain that they love their music but hate their instruments as much as they love them. Creative people in industry also show remarkable ambivalence toward their field.

I am reminded in this latter context of a talented engineer who achieved worldwide fame with his industrial innovation only to destroy the empire he had created, some fifteen years later, through a series of unwitting errors. At that point he sought analysis and was then able to discover that the crash had occurred when his financial success outstripped that of any member of his family for generations. The medium, whether paint, marble, words, the voice, the body, a musical instrument, or a social or political institution, will present itself as an ally as well as an enemy. The medium of creative expression has to be "tamed" so that the creator can impose upon it his or her will. This imposition must also obey two imperatives: it must translate the creator's inner vision but at the same time must carry the conviction that the chosen medium has the power to transmit to the external world the message, vision, or new concept in question.

The Innovator and the Public

The relation between the creative personality and the anonymous public is a love affair that bristles with hazards. The public to whom the message is directed is originally internal, composed of significant objects from the past which may be experienced as hostile or supportive. An unconscious battle must often be waged with this internal world before the work can be achieved. But the work still may not be considered worthy of being displayed. Not only do artists seek to impose upon the public their inner image but also they must be convinced that their creation has value, and that it is desired and appreciated by the public for whom it is intended. Creators and innovators frequently feel they must struggle with the external world for their right to display the most intimate expressions of their inner universe. Modell's reflection in chapter 3 on the "paradox of the private self and the social self" is evocative with regard to my own clinical work, particularly in the context of the artist and the outer world. A writer whom I shall quote later filled to the letter Modell's description of "the wish to be known and understood" counterbalanced by "the fear of being found and controlled."

The first question regarding severe blockage of the creative process concerns the nature of the fantasies that are projected onto the outer world: is it perceived as welcoming, admiring, desirous of receiving the creative offer or, on the contrary, as critical, rejecting, and persecutory? Such projections may be decisive with regard to permitting or refusing the "publication" of one's creative work, scientific research, or new invention. I find that I too often make remarks "out of the blue" (similar to those in the session quoted by Modell) in which both I and my analysand appear to be using projective and introjective identificatory processes. Recall that Bion considered communication through projective identification as a primitive or prototypic form of thinking.

THE INTERNAL WORLD

With regard to the inner world, I should like to review the importance of the pregenital and bisexual drives constantly revealed on the psychoanalytic stage and the extent to which these may prevent the artist's creative work from reaching the external world.

Pregenital Erotism and Archaic Sexual Impulses

The libidinal foundation of all creative expression is invariably infiltrated with pregenital impulses and archaic aspects of sexuality in which erotism and aggression, love and hate, are indistinguishable one from the other. The importance and richness of pregenital sexuality involves the five senses, as well as all bodily functions. However, certain senses, as well as certain zones and somatic functions, are frequently experienced unconsciously as forbidden sources of pleasure or as potentially dangerous acts and sensations.

To take into one's body and mind impressions received through any of the senses is in itself a creative act in any individual. The artist, in whatever field, is inevitably inspired by the external world, and once the impressions, perceptions, emotions, and thoughts thus garnered are incorporated mentally, their impact fertilizes the inner world of the creative mind. However, this perpetual movement between the two worlds may be experienced unconsciously as an orally devouring or destructive act.

A portrait painter comes to mind in regard to the repressed violence of oral impulses. This analysand, in spite of a strange abstract technique which had earned him a certain reputation, usually succeeded in capturing a likeness, but he would occasionally ruin portraits that were highly invested for him. We came to realize, after two years' analytic work, that in an omnipotent childlike manner, he held himself responsible for his mother's partially paralyzed face. We uncovered the fantasy that he was responsible for this paralysis. He was remembered as a greedy, demanding infant, difficult to feed and difficult to soothe, and it slowly became clear to both of us that he lived in terror of the explosive child within who had orally attacked and devoured his mother with his mouth and his eyes. In a sense he had spent his life trying, in magical ways, to repair this catastrophic damage. Reassurance from the family, explaining how his mother had come to suffer her affliction, did nothing to dispel the unconscious belief in his guilt. His portraits were explosive attacks upon the visual world, yet at the same time reparative in restoring a striking likeness to the individual portrayed.

A similar unconscious drama was revealed to me during the analysis of a plastic surgeon who claimed that his mother was an unusually ugly woman. On the few occasions when his professional work was not impeccably successful we were able to understand that he believed he had rendered his mother ugly and that any patient who reminded him of his mother made him excessively anxious. Yet he was able to invest, by means of a highly original surgical invention, the same violence that he had experienced in his early relationship with his mother. "I cut to cure," he announced. We were able to deconstruct this phrase and to understand that, through cutting, he satisfied different pregenital drives while at the same time making reparation for the fantasized damage of which he believed himself to be the author.

In the manner in which taking in from the environment may be feared as an orally destructive act, the activity of giving something of oneself to the outside world may in turn be experienced unconsciously as an act of defecation and therefore an agent of potential humiliation or destruction.

The first "creation" the infant offers to the external world is the fecal object, with all the erotic and aggressive meaning that is invariably associated with anal activity and fecal fantasy. This unconscious libidinal source plays a vital role for creative people in every domain. But the fantasies involved add an element of ambiguity in that fecal production is invariably experienced as referring to two distinct representations: on the one hand, it is something of great value, a gift offered to the world with love; on the other, it is a weapon, intended to attack and dominate the significant objects of the outer world. The unconscious nature of anal erotic and anal aggressive investments in the act of creation is, under-standably, an important determinant with regard to the capacity—or in-capacity—to continue producing, and to display one's productions to the world. When Schafer speaks of "orgasm being experienced by the ex-treme conformist as an anal explosion," this metaphor in my clinical ex-perience could also apply to the "creative orgasm" and, depending on the unconscious fantasies associated, may just as readily lead to severe inhi-bition of one's production.

In a similar vein the pleasure and excitement felt in the act of putting forth and rendering public one's production is also liable to be equated with exhibiting one's body or masturbating in public. Hanna Segal (1957) recounts the case of a musician who responded aggressively when she at-tempted to analyze his total inhibition with regard to playing in public. He told her that she was simply encouraging him to masturbate in front of the whole world. In her discussion of this episode Segal points out that the confusion of playing a musical instrument with a masturbatory act is not a true symbol but merely a "symbolic equivalent" in which internal and external reality are not distinguished from each other.

With regard to the bisexual wishes of infancy, posited by Freud as a universal given, observation of young children confirms that they tend to identify with both parents as well as desiring the privileges and magic powers of each for themselves. These omnipotent powers are usually symbolized by the parents' sexual organs. To the extent that both mas-culine and feminine wishes are well integrated and accepted, we all have the potentiality of being creative, through sublimating, so to speak, the impossible wish to be both sexes, and to create children with both par-ents. This may then permit us to produce parthenogenetic "infants" in the form of innovative works.

The three clinical vignettes that follow contain situations in which pregenital and bisexual wishes played a cardinal role in stimulating, as well as paralyzing, the creative process. It is my hope that these analytic fragments will throw further light on the inner universe of the creative individual as well as highlight unconscious reasons that inhibit the ca-pacity to create or to offer one's creation to the public.

PREGENITAL EROTISM AND CREATIVE EXPRESSION

Cristina, a sculptor from South America, was one of my first ana-lytic patients. She sought help many years ago during her art studies in Paris because she had reached a point of complete paralysis in her artis-tic production. She explained to me that although she dreamed of creat-ing monumental sculptures, she was only able to make very small con-structions; these, it turned out, were invariably sculpted in a fragile medium and were frequently chipped or broken—often by Cristina her-self. She spoke also of marital problems, as well as her fear that she was not a good mother to her two children (as though they too might be frag-ile and easily broken). Cristina also mentioned that she was incapable of showing her work publicly in spite of the encouragement of friends, among whom were a couple of gallery owners. The very thought of such an exhibition filled her with anxiety, induced insomnia, and brought her work to a complete halt.

The analysis was conducted four times a week and lasted six years. Cristina spent many sessions recalling her anguish concerning her body and its functions. This included lengthy exploration of intense mastur-bation guilt, stemming from childhood memories in which she had been severely chastised by her mother; she recalled being told that her auto-erotic activity would not only send Cristina to hell but would kill her mother. These memories led to our uncovering a hitherto unconscious fantasy that her own hands were imbued with destructive power, and that to exhibit her sculptures publicly would bring about her mother's death. In the first two years of our work together Cristina began to make larger pieces and to experiment with working in metal. She finally plucked up courage to enter a competition destined to promote young artists in all media. By coincidence, the theme of the competition for that year was "The Hand." Cristina constructed, in dark-colored material, a large ef-figy of her own hand. It was a strange and fascinating piece of work with something of the air of a prehistoric monster about it. "My sculpture has been chosen for exhibition," she announced one day and added, "Every-one will see it; and I've even sent my parents an invitation! My 'thing' will be displayed before the whole world and for once they will have to be proud of me." In the days that followed, she herself was able to put into words the belief that her "thing" was not only a symbolic reassurance of her bodily integrity but also announced the affirmation of sex and her right to feminine erotic pleasure.

In the years that passed since our analytic work terminated, I frequently received news from Cristina, and catalogues giving details of public showings of her work in Europe and abroad. A couple of years ago she called to say she was back in France for some time and needed an urgent appointment. She was once again suffering from massive anxiety which prevented her from sleeping and also from working. This outburst of panic had occurred on the opening night of an important exhibition of her work, large sculptures in stone and cement in quite a new style. We arranged that she would come once a week for several months.

In her first session she said: "I worked on the pieces for this show for over a year, and with a totally unusual feeling of freedom and pleasure which, as you know, is quite rare for me. There's always an anxious undercurrent just before a major exhibition but this time I wasn't aware of the slightest trace of panic. After the first night the publicity director remarked that my sculpts were unlike my former work, he said they were 'less austere' and also he noticed I had used a new technique that was, he said, 'quite unexpected of me.' I went home in a state of extreme anguish and collapse, such as I haven't known for years. For the last three weeks I've not been able to work, nor to sleep."

The following week I encouraged Cristina to tell me more about the new sculptures. "Well, there *is* something unusual about the present work. Not only did I truly enjoy creating it but I also added some decorative detail which would have been unthinkable for me, even two years ago. Now I'm filled with panic as soon as I enter my Paris atelier. I can't even think about work nor touch the piece I was working on."

In the week that followed, my curiosity, as well as my affectionate interest, led me to visit the exhibition, where I gazed upon the impressive pieces, overwhelming in their size and shape, but also highlighted with intriguing surface detail. I thought to myself how far Cristina's work had progressed from the timid little clay shapes of many years ago—and the extent to which it had also far surpassed the dramatic *Hand* which had been her breakthrough to the public.

In the sessions that followed, we recapitulated our discoveries of the past: the threat of death associated with masturbation, followed by an early memory from the age of three when her parents had gone away for a week, leaving her in the care of the maid. During this time she collected her feces and put them in a cardboard box in a cupboard in her bedroom. These were discovered by the maid, who scolded her severely and subsequently informed the parents of her crime. In a sense these had been Cristina's very first sculptures, in which she clung to her earliest gift to the outside world, presumably to stave off a feeling of loss and abandonment. There was an even earlier evocation in which Cristina remembered distinctly being carried naked by her nanny in front of a group of visitors. The nanny opened Cristina's legs and in a voice of disgust called everyone's attention to the fact that Cristina was urinating. This spectacle was greeted with loud laughter. Cristina thinks she was between a year and eighteen months of age. She had many times recaptured the feeling of urinating with pleasure only to be followed immediately by an intolerable sense of humiliation and public exposure.

During the session that followed this recapitulation, Cristina explained, for the first time, that the "decorative detail" with which she had adorned her recent sculptures had been added, after the initial casting, *by hand*. This new element led to a total re-evaluation of her exhibition, in which she recognized that history was repeating itself. Shortly before returning to her country she said, "I'm beginning to wonder if the extreme austerity that has always been the hallmark of my work was intended to mask my sexuality, and in fact to deny all sensuous body pleasure. My body functions have always made me feel anxious and guilty; and any sensuous feelings were invariably obscurely terrifying. Is it pleasure that is forbidden? The orgasm that must be denied at no matter what cost?"

I had observed during the initial period of our work together that when Cristina had begun to make ever larger sculptures and to use hard materials, this change coincided with the phase in which she could express verbally her feelings of rage toward the internal parents. The photographs she brought me of her work appeared at this time to incorporate and transmit some of this violent emotion. But with the return of her terror that her hands were murderous and liable to kill, the creative violence disappeared and the old inhibitions came back in force.

In this second period of analysis she was able to recall, for the first time, conversations in which her mother had given evidence of her personal rejection of sexual sensations and bodily pleasure of every kind. This led her to say, "My mother, whom I always believed to be a monster, has now became simply a psychologically sick, elderly lady." Following this crucial insight, in which Cristina was able to recognize a current of understanding and tenderness toward her mother, she began once again to create.

Whatever traumatic features from the past may have been reactivated in this sensitive artist, Cristina's anguish about her latest exhibition disappeared; within weeks she had signed a contract for a showing of the same work in another city and was anticipating the opening night with delight.

A further example of similar conflict but in another medium, was provided by Tamara, a violinist who was highly esteemed by the conservatory where she had been a prize-winning pupil (name and identifying details have been changed). Tamara suffered paralyzing anxiety when expected to perform in front of others; she would sometimes at the last minute cancel invitations to play at private musical evenings with friends or at concerts given by the pupils of the conservatory. After many months of research on her part as well as mine, in which we attempted to reconstruct the unconscious scenario that was being played out before every anticipated performance, she was able to capture the following fantasy: "I fool the world. My playing is far from the perfection I demand of myself, and people think I'm more talented than I really am. I scratch my instrument and instead of beauty all that comes out is excrement; as a musician I'm nothing but shit." Through recollections of shame and anguish attached to defecation during an encopretic period in infancy, Tamara came to understand that behind her terror of playing in public was not only the fear that she would exhibit what she believed to be an ugly and sexless body but that, behind the wish to give something valuable and beautiful to the public, there was a contrary desire: to drown the whole world with murderous feces. The extent to which she had projected onto her public the image of an angry, critical, and anally controlling mother was clearly revealed.

These insights enabled her to explore the feeling that she both loved and hated her musical instrument. Some months later she dreamed that she was reaching for her violin and her hands gave out light, which in turn illuminated the violin. In her associations she said with surprise, "You know, I've never realized that my violin is part of my own body. Even its shape is feminine!" When she was, for the first time in her memory, able to permit herself to love and caress her body, she at last felt free to contemplate exhibiting this extension of her bodily self to the outer world and began to anticipate that one day she might, with unambivalent affection, offer her musical gifts to the public. A year after the termination of her analysis she sent me two tickets for a concert in which she gave a most moving performance.

BISEXUALITY AND CREATIVITY

With regard to the role of primary bisexual drives in the creative process, it has always seemed to me that the pleasure experienced in intellectual and artistic achievements is infused with considerable narcissistic and homosexual fantasy; in such production, the individual is both man and woman at the same time. Perhaps all creative acts may be conceptualized as a fusion of the masculine and feminine elements in our psychic structure. Furthermore, clinical experience has taught me that conflicts over either of the two poles of homosexual libido—the wish to take over the mother's creative power as well as the father's fertile penis—may create serious inhibition or even total sterility in the capacity to put forth symbolic children in the form of intellectual and artistic creations. In the same vein, events that threaten to overthrow the delicate balance of bisexual fantasies in the unconscious mind may also precipitate inhibition of intellectual, scientific, and artistic capacities. From these notions it follows that any traumatic disturbance in somatic functioning, or any event that affects the sense of bodily integrity, can have a potentially profound influence on creative productivity.

A final analytic fragment highlights the role of bisexual wishes and the intimate link between the pregenital psychosexual body and creative expression, particularly when punishment for unconscious fantasies, impregnated with sexual and generative content, is projected onto the public.

A writer whom I shall call Benedicte originally sought help because her writing was completely blocked. As our work proceeded Benedicte uncovered two hitherto unconscious scenarios: that she must not create because her mother would take over or destroy anything she produced and the slow realization that her father (who had died when she was less than a year and a half old) had been the mainstay of her creativity but was felt to be forbidden as a figure of love. As she came to accept both her masculine and feminine identifications and the need to ensure for herself both parental functions, she began to write again. The first novel she produced (during our third year of analytic work) was chosen for a national television show devoted to promoting new young writers. When asked by someone on the panel how she explained the esoteric nature of her novel she replied: "It's because it's a story written by a child."

Three years later when her writing block seemed to have vanished entirely, Benedicte had to undergo an ovariectomy. Following this surgical operation she found herself, once again, unable to write, and feeling mutilated and as desperate as she had been six years earlier. A short extract from our analytic work a month after the operation illustrates the way in which the act of creation may be experienced as a dangerous transgression in that one has "stolen" the parents' generative powers. Benedicte said, "No one must know about my operation. It's another hideous secret like my father's death." Her mother had hidden the fact that the father was dead, telling the little girl, whenever she asked for her father, that he was "in the hospital." Benedicte discovered the truth by accident when she was five years old.

She goes on to make a link between her surgery and her father's operation for rectal cancer. A childlike part of her holds her mother responsible for his death, and through this bodily and deathlike link, she comes to reveal an unconscious fantasy that her mother is also responsible for her recent ovariectomy. In her associations it becomes clear that this aspect of the internalized mother is now fantasized as having attacked her sexuality and destroyed her capacity to bear children.

Benedicte is equally concerned in this session about two novels to which she cannot "give birth" at the present time. The title of one of them, "Which Crime for Which Criminal?" has led me to a number of free-floating hypotheses with regard to the nature of Benedicte's "crime." My first query was whether Benedicte, in typically childlike and megalomaniac fashion, unconsciously believed that she was responsible for having destroyed the parents' possibility of ever making another baby. This seemed a valid hypothesis in view of the fact that she was an only child and that her father had died when she was eighteen months old. As a result it may well be the small "criminal" Benedicte who believed that she no longer has the right to produce either books or babies.

After a long pause Benedicte recalls to mind a former lover, Adam, with whom she had once imagined she might have a baby. She continues: "They showed me the X-rays of my two ovaries. I have a fantasy that in one there was Adam's son and in the other his daughter. They had to be taken away from me of course!" I asked if these were the twin dolls that Benedicte had been given for her fifth birthday. One had been dressed as a boy and the other as a girl, and she played exclusively with the boy. One day her mother declared the dolls had to go to "the hospital," and when they came back, both were both girls. Such memories contributed to Benedicte's internal image of her mother as castrating and dangerous. "Yes! The twin dolls!" Benedicte said. "You know, she never wanted a daughter. All she ever wanted was a girl *doll!*"

Whatever her mother's pathology may have been, there is certainly an element of projection throughout the session, in that it is the *girl* who tends to imagine getting inside her mother's body and taking away all her feminine treasures: the babies, the father, and his penis. This common fantasy is now transformed in Benedicte's mind into the avenging mother who has destroyed Benedicte's ovaries so that she may not bear Adam's babies. When I point this out she says, "Yes, I can see that—but there's another problem, too. I'm afraid that if I put forth all my daydreams and book-children there'll be nothing left. I'll be completely emptied out."

Here is a further elaboration of the identical fantasy: that her creativity has been destroyed by the internalized mother-image, but with this difference—the metaphor now suggests a primitive fantasy of fecal loss. Benedicte has often recalled with irritation her mother's endless concern over bowel-functioning, which resulted in Benedicte's constantly receiving enemas. Her fantasy that there will be "nothing left" if she allows all her stories to come out suggests that it is no longer a question of her right to sexual and childbearing fulfillments but a *regressive* version of these, a fantasy of being emptied fecally by the anxious mother of childhood. She once again fears the loss of all her precious contents. In her reprojection of this unconscious fantasy, it is now the public that will empty her of her inner treasures.

The many dimensions that the anonymous public may represent for a writer are apparent. If Benedicte's books are unconsciously equated with children or feces, it is not surprising to discover that her public is felt to incorporate the most negative aspects of her representation of her mother—the one who will destroy all her inner contents.

Benedicte continues: "If I've started this last book the way I started my life, then of course I don't want my construction to stand. It has to fall down. *I'm not supposed to create!* Like the way I had to lose my ovaries. When it comes to giving birth then I have to abort. Am I being my own mother when she destroyed the first piece of writing I ever did? Must I destroy to fulfill my destiny?" Benedicte's associations indicate that her inability to create anything at the present moment is again due to her projection of destructive impulses onto the internal mother. She then says, "It's true that I'm holding back most of my 'contents.' I needed my father to protect me from her. And I know now that my writing springs from his presence in me. But my mother tried to get everything out of me as though all I had, all I was, belonged to her, not to me. So I'd die rather than give birth, or produce anything—for her!" After a long pause, she adds: "I torture myself with the idea that this present novel, the constipated one, won't be up to everybody's expectations. And I can't stand another rejection slip." We catch a final glimpse of the immense importance of public recognition as a factor in convincing creative people that they are *absolved* for their fantasized transgressions and pregenital erotism.

CONCLUDING REFLECTIONS

In the four situations outlined in this chapter—the struggle with the medium of expression; the struggle with projections upon the public; the force of pregenital drives; and the importance of psychic bisexuality—we are actually dealing with four versions of the primal scene, any or all of which may be a source of fertility, or of sterility. In addition to their libidinal attraction and the violent affect associated with each situation, the scenes are also experienced as forbidden or fraught with danger, either for the individual or for an anonymous other. There is probably no creative activity that is not unconsciously experienced as an act of transgression: one has dared to play alone through one's chosen medium of expression in order to fulfill secret libidinal, aggressive, and narcissistic aims; one has dared to display the resulting product to the outer world; one has dared to exploit pregenital sexuality with all its attendant ambivalence; and, finally, one has dared to steal the parents' generative organs and powers in order to make one's own creative offspring.

We can therefore appreciate that elements of humiliation, anger, and rage are of vital importance to creative production—as vital as are the elements of love and passion. It is understandable also that creative individuals are constantly subject to sudden disturbance or breakdown in their productivity when certain traumatic memories and primitive emotions from the past threaten to resurface and expose them to the "vengeance" of the external world. To conclude, the very traumas most closely associated with the psychosexual organization of the body-representation, as reflected by the significant objects of the past, are themselves at the origin not only of neurotic symptoms and inhibitions but of creativity itself.

REFERENCES

Freud, Sigmund. (1908). Creative writers and daydreaming. *Standard Edition* 9:143–153. New York: W. W. Norton, 1958.

Klein, Melanie. (1945). The Oedipus complex in the light of early anxieties. *International Journal of Psycho-analysis*, 26.

Pessoa, Fernando. (1989). *Poèmes Païens: d'Alberto Caeiro et de Ricardo Reis.* Paris: Bourgois.

Segal, Hanna. (1957). Notes on symbol formation. *International Journal of Psycho-analysis*, 38:391–397.

Winnicott, D. W. (1971). Playing: A theoretical statement. In: *Playing and Reality*. New York: Basic Books, 1971.

Otto F. Kernberg, M.D.

■ 6 Ideology and Bureaucracy as Social Defenses Against Aggression

REGRESSION AND DEFENSES AGAINST IT IN LARGE GROUPS

In earlier work (1980, chapter 11), I proposed that Turquet's (1975) description of the loss of a sense of identity in large groups constitutes the basic situation against which both the idealization of the leader of the horde described by Freud (1921) and the small-group flight-fight, dependency, and pairing processes described by Bion (1961) are defending. I have suggested that, owing to the nature of the regression that occurs in groups, group processes pose a basic threat to the members' personal identity, linked to a proclivity in group situations for the activation of primitive object relations, primitive defensive operations, and primitive aggression with predominantly pregenital features. These processes, particularly the activation of primitive aggression, are dangerous to the survival of the individual in the group, as well as to any task the group needs to perform.

To blindly follow the idealized leader of the mob, as described by Freud, reconstitutes a sort of identity by identification with the leader, permits protection from intragroup aggression by this common identity and the shared projection of aggression onto external enemies, and gratifies dependency needs by submission to the leader. The sense of power experienced by the individual identified with the mob of which he forms a part also gratifies primitive narcissistic needs. Paradoxically, the essentially irrational quality of mobs provides better protection against the painful awareness of aggression than what obtains in large-group situations with undefined external enemies, or in small groups, where it is hard to avoid being aware that the "enemy" is in the midst of the group itself.

The study of large-group processes highlights the threat to individual identity under social conditions in which ordinary role functions are suspended and various projective mechanisms are no longer effective. The relationships that exist among all individuals within a large-group situation replicate the multiplicity of primitive self- and object-representations that predominate as intrapsychic structures of the individual before the consolidation of ego, superego, and id—and, therefore, before the consolidation of ego identity—and the regressive features of part-object relations that evolve when normal ego identity is not achieved or disintegrates. Large-group processes also highlight the intimate connection between threats to retaining one's identity and fear that primitive aggression and aggressively infiltrated sexuality will emerge. My observations from the study of individual patients, of small groups, and of group processes in organizational and institutional life confirm, I believe, the overwhelming nature of the aggression evoked in unstructured group situations.

The point is that an important part of nonintegrated and nonsublimated aggression is expressed in vicarious ways throughout group and organizational processes. When relatively well-structured group processes evolve in a task-oriented organization, aggression is channeled toward the decision-making process, particularly by evoking primitive leadership characteristics in people in positions of authority. Similarly, the exercise of power in organizational and institutional life constitutes an important channel for the expression of aggression in groups that would ordinarily be under control in dyadic or triadic relations. Aggression emerges more directly and much more intensely when group processes are relatively unstructured.

In contrast to the dominant group characteristics of the unstable, threatening, potentially violent, and identity-diffusion–fostering quality of the large group, small-group formation deals with the idealization-persecution dichotomy in the respective activation of Bion's dependency and fight-flight groups. The activation of the pairing assumption may be considered an ambivalent effort to escape from primitive conflicts around aggression, primitive object relations, and primitive defenses by ambivalent idealization of the selected sexual pair.

PARANOID REGRESSION IN INSTITUTIONS

The two most striking mechanisms by which the large group protects itself from the threat of impending aggression are the development of an ad hoc ideology and/or a process of bureaucratization. The development of a simplistic philosophy as a calming, reassuring doctrine that reduces all thinking to obvious clichés described by Turquet (1975), the primitive, narcissistic ego ideal characteristic of large-group processes described by Anzieu (1984), and the narcissistic ideology and idealization of a pseudo-paternal leader as "promoter of illusions" described by Chasseguet-Smirgel (1984) all refer to the tendency toward a narcissistic regression into a primitive ideology that transforms the large group into what Canetti (1960) described as the typical "feasting crowd," engaged, we might say, in dependent and narcissistic behavior and a corresponding search for a calming, narcissistic, reassuring mediocrity in its leader. Such leadership never fails to appear. I have described such regression as characteristic of the mass psychology of conventionality (1989), reflecting the type of ideology characteristic of a latency child's superego and represented typically by mass entertainment.

Instead of such a static crowd, the large group may alternatively evolve into a dynamic mob characterized by predominantly paranoid features and selection of paranoid leadership, typically represented by the mass psychology of revolutionary mass formations. Conventionality, on the one hand, and violent, revolutionary movements with a totalitarian ideology, on the other, may be considered the corresponding mass psychological outcomes of idealization and persecution as basic group phenomena, and either the containment of aggression by denial and reaction formation or its expression by violent acting out.

Having outlined the release of aggression under conditions of regressed and unstructured group processes, I now wish to explore conditions under which the development of pathological aggression occurs in the context of institutional functioning and malfunctioning, and the vicissitudes of ideology and bureaucracy as protective and corrective measures against the outbreak of aggression.

In earlier work, following Elliot Jacques's (1976) classification of social organizations into requisite (functional) and paranoiagenic (dysfunctional) ones, I explored the nature of paranoiagenic organizations (1993), expanding on Jacques's description of them as characterized by the prevalence of suspicion, envy, hostile rivalry, and anxiety, with a breakdown of social relationships regardless of how much individual good will there might be. I suggested that institutional paranoiagenesis ranges along a broad spectrum from the psychopathic to the depressive. Under conditions of paranoiagenic regression in nonrequisite functioning organizations, the psychopathic end of the spectrum is characterized by members who manifest patently deceptive, dishonest, antisocial behaviors that they would not evince in their daily lives outside the institution. And members who show antisocial tendencies throughout all their social interactions and who also manifest those tendencies in their organizational life are not only accepted but are admired for getting away with their antisocial behavior.

The average members of the organizations led by such people evince, in contrast, markedly paranoid features in their institutional dealings that contrast with their normal personality characteristics outside organizational life. Paranoid behaviors constitute a middle range of the spectrum of paranoiagenic regression and are the most prevalent manifestations of the dysfunctional nature of the organization. Typically, the relationship of the staff or the employees to the supervisors and the leaders is characterized by fear, suspicion, and resentment, a sense of hyperalertness and cautiousness, a search for subtle and hidden meanings and messages, and an effort to establish alliances with peers to defend against what are perceived as common dangers. These developments cause the leader to feel that paranoid members of the organization have begun to challenge his legitimate authority through defiant attacks implicitly condoned by a silent majority.

At the depressive end of the spectrum of an institution characterized by paranoiagenic regression, individual members typically feel lonely, isolated, unappreciated, and hypercritical about their own faults and shortcomings. They overreact to criticism, experiencing it as threats to their professional future in the organization. Their exaggerated self-criticism inhibits their work functions, thus creating self-perpetuating cycles that interfere with work performance and work satisfaction and lead to efforts to escape from the organization. Not surprisingly, the most mature members of the organization (those with the most integrated superegos) predominate among those with the depressive reaction. Normal people in paranoiagenic institutions become the most alienated from it. Schizoid withdrawal is another possible defense.

The causes of organizational paranoiagenesis include: (1) the breakdown of the task systems of organizations when their primary tasks become irrelevant or overwhelming or are paralyzed by unforeseen, undiagnosed, or mishandled constraints; (2) the activation of regressive group processes under conditions of institutional malfunctioning; and (3) the latent predisposition to paranoid regression that is a universal characteristic of individual psychology. Faulty organizational leadership may be the major cause of the breakdown of task performance, even when external reality would foster the successful carrying out of the organization's primary tasks and even when no major constraints to such primary tasks exist objectively. Faulty leadership may derive from the personality characteristics of leaders in key administrative positions. Indeed, all breakdown in organizational functioning, with its consequent regression in the group processes throughout the organization, initially looks as if the troublesome personalities of key leaders were responsible. Only a careful organizational analysis may differentiate those cases in which the leader's psychopathology is actually the cause of the organizational breakdown from those in which his pathology is only a presenting symptom, reflecting regression in leadership that is secondary to organizational breakdown, rather than its cause.

The most frequent cause of paranoia in social organizations is the limitation, and particularly a reduction in, the resources available for carrying out the organizational tasks. At times of budgetary constraints, for example, waves of apprehension and objective anxiety are compounded by individual members' regression to primitive anxieties of being abandoned, rejected, discriminated against, and unfairly exploited. Insofar as promotions also imply competition for a diminishing number of positions as individual members ascend the administrative ladder, a struggle for limited resources occurs. When competition involves search committees, comparative judgments about the value of individual members for the organization, and a political process influencing such appointments, it is no longer simply a matter of distributing resources but of adding a new dimension, politics, to the conditions favoring paranoia.

The definition of politics viewed in terms of organizational functioning may be narrowed to behavior carried out by individuals or groups to influence other individuals or groups in the pursuit of their interests or goals. Masters's (1989) definition of institutional politics is most apt: "a form of rivalry to determine which humans are permitted to transmit 'authoritative' messages or commands to the rest of society." When political action derives from goals linked to an organization's primary tasks, it may be considered essentially functional and rationally related to organizational functioning. However, when political action is tangential or unrelated to functional institutional goals, it has negative effects on institutional task systems and task boundaries and may lead not only to significant distortions in institutional functioning but also to an increase in conditions favorable to paranoia.

If authority is defined as the functional exercise of power within an institutional setting, the exercise of power as part of a political process that has no connection to institutional tasks cannot be called functional. And if the exercise of power is not functional, a spectrum of institutional dysfunctioning results, ranging from chaos when insufficient power is located at points of functional authority, to petrification when excessive power is located with institutional leaders, transforming authority into authoritarianism.

In terms of group processes within an institution, politicizing always results in an increased dependence of all members on all others; the anonymous members of the organization all carry potential political decision-making power, a situation maximized under conditions of democratic decision making. To depend on all others when conditions are not objectively regulated by organizational structures immediately activates large-group functioning. The political process thus immediately activates the psychology of large-group regression, with the consequent loss of personal identity on the part of all involved, a vague sense of threatened aggression and violence, feelings of impotence, a need to form subgroups so that aggression can be projected onto other groups, an effort to assert personal and small-group power over others, a fear of being victimized by the same process, a wish to escape from the situation, and a sense of paralysis and impotence as one disengages from the large group.

A lack of correspondence between an organization's objectives and its actual administrative structure is an important but often neglected source of conditions fostering paranoia. The most typical examples of those unrecognized discrepancies are institutions that officially exist to perform a social function for the common good, whereas the actual primary function is to provide jobs and satisfactions for their constituent bureaucracies. Other structural faults, distortions, or inadequacies include a lack of clear and stable boundary control on the part of managerial leadership, inadequate, ambiguous, or overlapping delegation of authority, and a discrepancy between the authority delegated to particular leaders and the actual power given to them. This last may derive from organizational problems or a failure in individual leaders. Incompetence in leaders not only has a devastating effect on organizational functioning but also is enormously paranoiagenic. Incompetent leaders, when protecting themselves against competent subordinates, become highly distrustful, defensive, and deceptive; they become authoritarian toward subordinates and subservient toward superiors, both of which activate paranoiagenic regression, particularly its paranoid and psychopathic aspects.

As a consequence of these processes and structural characteristics, regressive group processes and the corresponding activation of primitive aggression activate the latent disposition in members of the organization for regression to preoedipal levels of intrapsychic organization. At those levels the projection of aggression onto parental figures, the reintrojection of such parental figures under the distorted consequences of projected aggression, and the consequent circular reaction of projection and introjection of aggression are dealt with by massive splitting mechanisms, leading to idealization, on the one hand, and to paranoid, persecutory tendencies, on the other hand. Those psychic operations, having their origin in the dyadic relationship with the mother, also resonate with triangular problems reflecting the oedipal situation and transform the disposition toward preoedipal transferences into the typical triangular oedipal ones that become dominant in the individual's relationship with authority.

The distortion of rational authority resulting from these projective processes leads to defensive activation of narcissistic affirmation and to regressive relationships with feared or idealized parental leaders. The process is completed by a general tendency to reproject the advanced aspects of superego functioning onto the total institution, in parallel to Freud's (1921) description of the characteristics of mass psychology. The projection of superego functions onto the institution at large increases the subjective dependence on the institution's evaluation of the member, decreases his or her capacity to rely on internalized value systems, and provides the direct trigger for the individual's contamination by ideological cross currents and rumors; regression into primitive depressive and persecutory anxieties occurs when objective feedback and reassurance in the organization fail. Under those conditions there is a threat of not only emotional and characterological regression but moral regression as well. The paranoid urge to betray (Jacobson, 1971) is a logical consequence of that regression.

BUREAUCRACY

The most important means by which organizations can protect themselves against producing paranoia and contain the aggression that may be activated in large-group processes is to establish a bureaucratic system. A bureaucracy, as Jacques (1976) has argued, can provide rationally determined hierarchies, public delineation of responsibility and accountability, stable delegation of authority, and an overall accountability of the organization to its social environment by both legal and political means and a parallel organization of employees and labor unions. Essential to optimal bureaucratic functioning is that the institution be accountable to or controlled by the state or by law. A well-functioning bureaucracy in a democratic system has the potential for being an ideal model of organizational structure.

Masters (1989) summarized the principal characteristics of the bureaucracy. First, it provides an element of coercion, which is necessary for large groups of people with conflicting interests if they are to function for the benefit of all. Second, by creating new ways of cooperation among constituent groups, the bureaucracy has the potential for increasing efficiency. Third, bureaucracies provide benefits for their members, thus enhancing their self-perpetuation.

Within bureaucratic organizations or institutions, internal conflicts can be diagnosed, controlled, and rationally resolved by standard mechanisms of bureaucratic functioning. Bureaucratic structure reduces the

regression into large-group processes in organizations and, under ordinary circumstances, keeps paranoiagenic regression at a low level. Effective bureaucratic functioning may make for optimal task performance,
maintain normal social exchange in an institution, and impose firm compliance with what is generally assumed to be the common good. Bureaucracies may use resources effectually, and the participants may find
their work gratifying.

There are, however, important limitations to the ameliorating effects
of bureaucratic functioning. Those limitations, I believe, arise from the
unavoidable infiltration of aggression in the form of dissociated sadism
into all group processes. That infiltration affects all institutional functioning, including the performance of functional tasks.

There are multiple mechanisms by which a bureaucratic structure
may lend itself to express the aggression that is generated but cannot
be acknowledged by all members of an organization. Inadequate leaders
of a bureaucratic structure, particularly a leader with severely narcissistic and/or paranoid tendencies, may transform a bureaucratic system
into a social nightmare. Such leaders expect and foster subservient behaviors from their subordinates, reward the idealization of the leadership, and are prone to persecute those whom they sense to be critical of
them.

Mechanisms at the periphery of bureaucratic systems tend to increase
the size and scope of operations beyond what is functionally warranted,
and they gradually deteriorate. As Masters (1989) pointed out, equal justice for all implies that any particular person may feel dehumanized and
neglected by bureaucracies. In fact, those negative aspects of bureaucratic systems may be the first effects on the lives of persons who enter
the organization, leading to efforts to beat the system and to escape from
its rigidities, which in turn leads to a paranoid reaction by the bureaucrats to catch the cheaters. Efforts to humanize the system and to do
somebody a good turn may, however, lead to favoritism—particularly to
nepotism—and may bring about the corruption of the system.

The gradual expansion of a bureaucratic system to protect itself further against actual or potential cheaters may lead to a bureaucratic over-

growth that affects not only individuals but the entire institution. Functional administrative leaders may have to find ways to cut through intolerable bureaucratic rigidities for optimal task performance. In short, the dangers of rigidification, and/or chaotic breakdown (as corruption gains the upper hand), constitute the major limits to the potentially corrective effects that bureaucratic systems may have in preventing the developing of paranoia.

When bureaucracies grow to such an extent that they dominate the society of which they are a part, their self-serving functions become manifest: the bureaucrats become a privileged class who use the payoff to placate the underprivileged they "serve." The bureaucracy is no longer functional; its petrified and chaotic features serve its own interests. Here paranoia seems a justified response by all concerned, both inside and outside the bureaucracy. As I pointed out in earlier work (Kernberg, 1994), the economic breakdown of the Soviet Union found its most dramatic expression in the development of a parasitic bureaucracy that combined rigidity with widespread corruption and contributed to the high level of paranoia in that society even as political terror itself decreased.

A less apparent, subtle, and yet prevalent deterioration in bureaucratic organizations stems from the assignment of particular members as gatekeepers or inspectors to protect the common good against potentially unjustified demands, expectations, appointments, or privileges. Inspectors of municipal, state, or federal regulatory agencies and the chairpersons of committees deciding on the selection of personnel, the adequacy of the documentation of various requests, the distribution of resources of any kind, the authorization for various permits, and the evaluation of people inside and outside the bureaucratic structure are unconsciously invested with the dissociated sadism that is prevalent throughout the total organization. In other words, all the narcissistic and paranoid tendencies that in ordinary social interactions are controlled by means of the bureaucratic structure are perversely placed onto the guardians of the gate. Those guardians, under the guise of objective justice, are frequently victims of that role suction and become grandiose (narcissistic), sadistic, and suspicious (paranoid) arbiters of human destiny. The impotence of persons ordinarily restricted in their scope of autonomous decision making by an immense bureaucratic system may foster in them an explosion of narcissistic needs when such opportunities for power are made available; the arbitrariness and the sadism with which individual bureaucrats—particularly those in subordinate positions—may treat the public is proverbial.

Those of us who have had to deal with such emissaries from overarching bureaucratic systems as part of our leadership functions in health delivery systems can offer numerous examples of such a massive outburst of sadistic behavior on the part of inspectors, surveyors, and site visitors. One major—and on a social scale devastating—effect of the bureaucracy's need to justify and expand its own functions is the generation of essentially nonfunctional, redundant work, thus adding enormous although almost invisible costs to the functioning of social organizations. The New York Hospital Association has calculated that 25 percent of the total expense budget of hospitals is consumed by the need to respond to bureaucratic requests of one kind or another (McCarthy, 1978).

Even without any particular ideological underpinnings, the rationale and justification of bureaucratic rigidities usually include one of three proverbial statements: "We have always done it this way," "We have never done it this way," or "If we do this, everybody will be able to come and get (away with) it." When, in addition, bureaucratic requirements are justified or infiltrated by an ideological system, the sadistic, moralistic, and punitive effects of bureaucratic action may assume objectively persecutory features.

The terrible consequences of the effective functioning of bureaucracies in totalitarian states, such as Hitler's Germany and Stalin's Soviet Union, on the ordinary lives of large segments of the population requires no spelling out. To a limited degree, similar types of ideological infiltration of well-functioning bureaucracies may be encountered within democratic states as well. In the United States, it is probably within the regulatory systems affecting health, education, welfare, immigration, and, particularly, justice that ideological infiltration on bureaucratic control systems may have a maximum effect of reducing efficiency, generating

parasitic work, and restricting individual freedom and ordinary social interactions while increasing the paranoiagenic, persecutory regulation of
the social system. It is probably because of the immediate visibility of cost
increases in the private sector of industry that its bureaucratic regulations
are constrained in a dynamic equilibrium with the pressure for efficiency.

For example, within the bureaucratic hypertrophy of the judicial system, Salvador Menuchin (personal communication, 1994) has pointed to
the disastrous effects of standard bureaucratic policies in the court system in dealing with child neglect and child abuse. The appointment of
independent legal counsel to the child and to the parent, in addition to
the authority of the judge, and the treatment of each neglected child
within a dysfunctional family as a separate court case, all combine to
siphon an enormous amount of resources into legal proceedings, limit
the authority of health system agencies concerned with the child and the
entire family, and increase family conflicts by injecting into them a legal
adversary system.

The expression of envy, within large-group psychology, toward individuals whose capacity for independent thinking and autonomous functioning is resented within such a regressive group situation, is replicated
in the bureaucratic suspicion of innovative solutions to a particular problem connected with the realm of authority of that bureaucracy. The manifest resentment of such original solutions on the part of the bureaucrats
finds a troubling, yet not surprising, resonance within the disaffected
membership of a regressed institution that resents the creative task performance of its own leadership. The proverbial anonymous letters of dis-
gruntled employees sent to regulating agencies are more often than not
part of this psychology. Less frequently, they may reflect an outburst of
impotence from the healthy subordinates at the periphery of a paranoiagenic organization.

IDEOLOGY

Bureaucratic hypertrophy may also relate to ideology in more
complex though equally destructive ways. Ideology refers to a system

of beliefs that a group, a mass, or a society share regarding the origin and functions of their common social life and the cultural and ethical demands and expectations they aspire to. Here I wish to point to the existence of significant discrepancies between a society's ideological commitments and the financial means to fulfill such commitments. Bureaucratic requirements mandating services that society cannot afford or is not willing to pay for may reflect an unconscious compromise formation between ideological commitment and practical considerations. The destructive effects of bureaucratic persecution of agencies such as hospitals, which are supposed to produce services without adequate financial coverage, leads to a worsening of the financial crisis by the nonfunctional work generated through these additional bureaucratic pressures.

Underlying these contradictions lies the relationship, in our democratic society, between the ideological aspirations of liberty, equality, and justice for all. These are geared to contain aggression at a social level but may become instrumental in the very acting out of that aggression. A humanistic ideology that has at its center the respect for the individual and individual rights and the aspiration for equal opportunity and equality before the law—an ideology embedded in a democratic system of government—may support the social controls that protect the functioning of organizational structures, guarding organizations against the corruption of leaders and the paranoiagenic deterioration derived from the misuse of power.

However, the same ideology may be subverted by the regressive atmosphere created in the context of large-group processes. Individual rights may be perverted within a litigious culture that artificially inflates grievances. Paranoid grandiosity becomes rationalized as individual rights. The quest for equality may be a rationalization of unconscious envy generated under conditions of regressive group processes. Zinoviev (1984) pointed to the importance of an egalitarian ideology as part of Soviet Marxism in fostering the group's envy of anybody who would assume leadership, and the unconscious self-assurance derived from the selec-

tion of mediocrities to leadership functions as a way to assuage such ide-
ologically reinforced envy. I have already referred to the selection of narcissistic mediocrities as a central aspect of the transformation of the
large-group situation into a static satisfied group that depends on the narcissistic leader.

In this regard, social ideologies tangential to institutional functioning
often have a destructive effect on that functioning, particularly through
the skillful misuse of the ideology by individual members of the institution—a painful side effect of well-intentioned efforts for the socially
mandated and protected redress of grievances. The very ideal of a democratic system of government may misfire when this ideal inspires another major mechanism to control the development of paranoia, namely,
a democratic process of decision making. Such a democratic process includes the open discussion of issues that affect everybody; the assurance
of equal rights for open communication at all levels of the hierarchy; the
public, stable, and socially sanctioned distribution of authority on a functional basis; and the full participation of all followers in the selection of
their leaders.

Here, unfortunately, paranoiagenic effects may result from two major
causes: the nature of political processes and a generally shared confusion
between democratic and functional mechanisms of decision making.
Democracy is a political system of government that, in essence, is opti-
mally geared to social regulation in open societies (or, in systems terms,
in open systems with an infinite number of boundaries). In contrast, limited social organizations such as schools, hospital, factories—that is,
open systems with a limited number of boundaries and specific tasks that
have to be carried out to assure the survival of that organization—require
functional leadership that corresponds to the task systems that enable the
organization to carry out its mission. This distinction between functional
and democratic decision making is absolutely crucial in social organizations with concrete tasks and functional management.

Functional decision making, however, involves participatory management—that is, the possibility of group discussions and joint decision

making among leaders at any particular hierarchical level. If participatory management coincides with a clear and stable delegation of authority to each group involved in such collective decision making and if the individual authority of leaders is commensurate with their responsibilities—authority may be delegated but the responsibility cannot—such a functional organization may appear to be democratic, but it corresponds, rather, to the functional principles of social organization.

Returning once more to a humanistic ideology that puts respect for the individual at the center of its concerns, an apparently simple, sometimes highly effective, but also easily subvertible mechanism of reducing the development of paranoia is represented by well-motivated persons with integrity, concern for the organization and the human values enacted in it, who reach across organizational boundaries and task systems to help somebody in trouble. This can be accomplished by bringing together two adversaries to straighten out their conflict or talking extensively with one person caught up in a paranoid, self-perpetuating web of misconception. Gathering a significant group of peers to present to their superiors the problems that they are ignoring or mismanaging can be helpful. Individual courage, the normal sense of commitment to values, and altruistic drive can move individual members to transcend paranoiagenic regression. Such an approach to institutional management can broaden the awareness of paranoia, its universal nature, and the importance of activating corrective measures to deal with it.

However, that corrective process, with the best intention in the world, may also be subverted destructively. Individual decency and high moral values may be corrupted by being combined with naivete, that is, with an unconscious denial of the aggressive and sadistic temptations of members in group functioning. In open institutions where feedback is encouraged and a functional organization prevails, persons with antisocial tendencies are able to circulate false information that acquires weight precisely because of the mutual respect of all involved. The emergence in leadership positions of those with strong paranoid, narcissistic, or antisocial characteristics may in itself indicate the degree of regression of the group processes in the organization: the degree of prominence of paranoid persons in the group process at any particular time may be considered an indirect indicator of the extent to which a paranoiagenic atmosphere prevails.

Let us examine some of the characteristics of ideological systems. Some of these counteract the regressive pull that occurs in unstructured groups. Others may foster a regressive enactment of aggression in groups leading to the "return of the repressed," the enactment of aggression in the form of violence, sadistic power, and constraint of individual liberties.

From a psychoanalytic viewpoint, one characteristic is the extent to which an ideological system includes a world view that, by definition, excludes all those who do not share that view, declares them to be enemies who must be controlled or eliminated, and aspires to dominate all aspects of social behavior. This characteristic, which may be called the paranoid pole of ideologies, is found in totalitarian societies, fundamentalist religious movements, and certain cults. The division of all human beings into either loyal adherents or dangerous enemies may also be found in some racist and nationalist ideologies. A second characteristic of such ideologies is their invasiveness of family and intimate relationships, including their supraordinate control over the relationships of the couple, typically matched by an intolerance toward sexuality as described by Freud (1921). Family and sexual intimacy threaten the individual's complete identification with a totalitarian ideology. A third general characteristic of such totalitarian ideologies is usually a remarkable conventional and conformist set of moral principles regulating individual behavior, reminiscent of the superego of the latency years. Fundamentalist religious groups focus this morality most specifically on the sexual behavior of the individual—in effect mounting a massive defense against individual freedom in integrating eroticism and tenderness.

At the opposite end of the spectrum of ideological regression—what may be called the narcissistic pole of ideologies—we find the transformation of ideologies into social, political, and religious clichés that maintain their function of socialization within the community but have remarkably little effect on the daily functioning of the individual, the couple, and the community. I am referring here, for example, to the ritualized participation in official, national, religious, or ethnic celebrations, maintaining form rather than commitment to a particular ideology, all of which may include both benign ritualization of social interactions and a reflection of a historical, racial, or religious tradition. A particular type of such formalistic and essentially empty ideology is what may pervade a totalitarian society, the reality of the daily life of which is in striking contradiction to the corresponding ideological system. A cliché-ridden adherence to the ideology illustrates the loss of individual liberties as well as the split between a dishonest public life and a grim private life. Kolakowski (1978), Voslensky (1983), Sinyavsky (1988), and Malia (1994) have described these characteristics of Soviet Russia as typical of its social structures during the thirty years before its collapse.

Intermediate between these two extremes of ideology formation we might place ideological systems characterized by the following features or having evolved to these characteristics at some stage of their history. Here the ideology is typically based on a general humanistic value system within which the individual's rights and responsibilities are stressed, the responsibilities linked to moral demands expressed in his or her relationship to the community, and the individual's internal set of ethical values, potential differences among individuals, and the right of privacy in decisions regarding family and couple relationships are respected. Within these kinds of ideologies, equality of rights is stressed, assured by equality before and access to the law, with a tolerance for differences of lifestyle, that is, without an imposition of an ideological egalitarianism that would significantly restrict individual freedom of decision making.

I must stress that such a spectrum of ideologies, ranging from cliché-ridden rituals, at one extreme, to violent, restrictive totalitarianism, at the other, with a humanistic central domain, may include the same theoretical system, the same ideology operating at different levels of regression. Thus, for example, the cliché-ridden "pseudo-Marxism" characteristic of the Soviet Union and its satellite states may be considered the counterpart to the paranoid ideologies of Marxist terrorist groups in

Germany, Peru, Cambodia, and the Middle East, and the intermediate "Marxism with a human face" reflected in the ideology of some reform Communist movements in Eastern and Western Europe. Similar observations may be made regarding religious systems that range throughout this entire spectrum in their various manifestations. The general implication of this description of ideological polarities is that the paranoid ideologies act out the aggression against which the ideology emerged as a defense: the combination of paranoid ideologies and well-functioning bureaucracies may be extremely dangerous to human survival. The effective bureaucracy, under these circumstances, may transform an open society into a political state.

Now we may explore the individual's contribution to the level of ideological maturity or regression that he or she adopts as a consequence of the development of individual superego functions. Here we also have a spectrum ranging from the primitive, sadistic, conventional morality of the classical "authoritarian personality," at one extreme, to the cynical manipulation of socially accepted belief systems of the individual with severe antisocial tendencies, at the other, the individual with a mature superego occupying the central domain of this spectrum.

In fact, the individual's fixation at a level of a primitive superego reflects both severe character pathology and a remarkable consonance with the characteristics of fundamentalist ideologies. An individual with this fixation divides values into "all good" and "all bad," aspires for an individual "justice" that reflects a system of rationalized envy and hatred of others' rights and belongings, and adopts a sexual morality with an absolute split between tender and erotic relations. The point is that, while social, cultural, historical, and economic conditions may determine the level of ideological commitments sweeping a culture, the individual's psychopathology or maturity of superego functions will determine if and where such an individual enters the historical current.

PSYCHOANALYTIC AND SOCIOLOGICAL CONVERGENCES

In the final part of this chapter, I shall summarize some of the conclusions derived from the proceeding ideas and relate them to corresponding views derived from the classical sociological tradition. I have proposed that the psychology of small groups, large groups, mobs, and mass movements includes the expression, under conditions of unstructured social interactions, of primitive aggression and defenses against it that are ordinarily under control in the restricted dyadic and triadic relationships of individuals, couples, and, to some extent, families. The relationships within ordinary social networks that characterize communities also reflect in large part the dyadic and triadic relationships within which both primitive aggression and defenses against it are under control.

In contrast, in response to the liberation of primitive aggression in the group situations referred to, a tendency also exists toward the activation of regressive narcissistic and paranoid developments. Narcissistic developments predominate in the static, gratifying, although also simplifying and at times stultifying enjoyment of group regression and the corresponding relationship to narcissistic, primitive, cliché-ridden leadership. Paranoid regression, on the other hand, is characterized by the dynamic mob, mass movement, and the corresponding liberation of violence and elimination of ordinary moral constraints described by Freud (1921). Under conditions of paranoid regression, leadership with paranoid characteristics is in ascendance and provides direction, rationalization, and encouragement for the expression of destructiveness.

I have suggested that, in addition to ordinary task orientation—the structural transformation of groups into organized task or work groups within institutions—two major alternative defensive operations against the activation of aggression are represented by bureaucratic control and ideology formation. Bureaucratic control develops a structure of a kind, protects the individual, the group, and the organization against regressive effects of paranoid developments, and, at a broader social level, may protect individual rights as well as equality before the law. An ideological development that unifies the unstructured group or mass movement in terms of a relatively simple set of moral prescriptions also provides a defense against paranoid regression and the outbreak of violence.

Both bureaucratic development and ideology, however, may be infiltrated by the very aggression that they are geared to defend against. Bureaucratic control may acquire regressive sadistic qualities; ideological systems can develop the rationalization of violence and totalitarian control. Thus, major defenses against aggression may actually become infiltrated by it and reinforce the enactment of aggression. Ideology and bureaucracy may reinforce each other at both regressive and advanced levels. An ideology of egalitarianism may foster a hypertrophic bureaucracy to ensure that egalitarianism, paradoxically creating a privileged bureaucratic class and reducing individual freedoms. A libertarian ideology of individual rights may explode into a legalistic bureaucracy that transforms the defense of individual rights into a litigious and querulous relationship between individuals and the social system. While it is easy to assert that restriction of bureaucratic development and protection of humanistic ideology may together protect social life from the dangerous excesses of bureaucratic and ideological developments, it would be extremely naive to assume that this is an easy task. In fact, I believe that this dilemma presented by human aggression at a social level probably requires constant alertness rather than any particular permanent solution.

The positive aspect both of bureaucratic development and ideological commitments have to be kept in mind. The mass demonstrations and spontaneous uprisings in Eastern Europe against Communist totalitarianism and the spontaneous mobilization of the British people in response to the massive bombardments in the early stages of the Second World War are illustrations of mass movements combining a humanistic ideology with collective courage. Here the positive aspects of ideological commitment have produced positive historical change and stemmed the effects of destructive aggression at a social, national, and international level. Similarly, the support provided by bureaucratic structures for individuals by setting up avenues for redress of grievances, and the possibility of optimal functioning of task systems within and across social institutions are an essential aspect of the social organization of human work.

But the ever present dangers of ideological regression and bureaucratic sadism cannot be overestimated. Within our own society, the relationship between a humanistic ideology of personal freedom and equality, on the one hand, and a hypertrophic tendency toward litigious interactions and restrictive "political correctness," on the other, indicate the problem referred to at the level of ideology formation. The vast, largely undiagnosed, hypertrophic bureaucratic restrictions in the area of health care are a typical expression of the evident contradiction between egalitarian aspirations and growing economic constraints derived from the very development of scientific knowledge and effectiveness of health care procedures.

Tocqueville (1835–40) first pointed to the danger that democracy could become a plebicitarian tyranny, under the effect of the transformation of public opinion into despotic laws and bureaucratic structures. He clearly foresaw the risk that the aspirations for equality can eventually reduce individual freedoms, although he had strong confidence in the social checks and balances he found in the United States, such as the independence of the judiciary, the separation of religion and state, the autonomy and high status of the professions, the authority of local community, and regional diversity (Nesbit, 1993).

This view was in dramatic contrast to that of Marxist theory, which assumed that the dictatorship of the proletariat, in bringing about the destruction of the bourgeoisie and the capitalist system, would by itself "disappear" and give rise to universal freedom (Kolakowski, 1978). The development within the Soviet system of a totalitarian and corrupt bureaucracy (the *Nomenklatura*) (Voslensky, 1983) illustrates both a fatal flaw in Marxist thinking and the danger of bureaucratization affecting both the socialist and democratic systems.

Weber's (1904–05) analysis of bureaucracy saw the rational organization of government and the economy as expressed in bureaucracy as a form of rational domination, a mode of hierarchy that supplants patrimonial, charismatic, and/or traditional authority by means of principles of fixed and official jurisdictional areas, governed by laws or administrative regulations. He foresaw potential conflicts between democracy and bureaucracy, with bureaucracy subverting the moral objectives of democracy. Michels (1911) suggested, in his description of bureaucracy:

"The bureaucratic spirit corrupts character and engenders moral poverty. In every bureaucracy we may observe place-hunting, a mania for promotion, an obsequiousness toward those on whom promotion depends; there is arrogance toward inferiors and civility toward superiors. . . . We may even say that the more conspicuously a bureaucracy is distinguished by its zeal, by its sense of duty, and by its devotion, the more also will it show itself to be petty, narrow, rigid, and illiberal" (p. 189).

Durkheim (1893, 1925) concluded that only moral systems linking the individual to his immediate community could protect the individual from the destructive effects of authoritarian bureaucracies depending upon the state; he saw the potential of mutual corrective influences in the protection of individual freedom by the role of the individual, his moral systems linking him with the community and the state. As Nesbit (1993) points out, Tönnies's (1887) analysis of the distinction between community and society underlies all the sociologists' analysis referred to so far (with the exception of Marx). Tönnies conceived of the dangers that community, with its specific moral systems, might be supplanted by society, that is, by a vast, atomized transformation of the relations of individuals among each other, related to the democratic system of government. This puts at risk the moral systems of the community by the impersonal transformation of society at large. Kolakowski (1978) traced the contradictions in the Soviet system back to a paradox in the ideals of the French revolution: liberty, equality, fraternity. He pointed to the fact that absolute liberty denies equality, while absolute equality cannot but deny liberty; the conflict between these two ideals destroys fraternity as well.

I started from a psychoanalytic perspective of group psychology, which led me to the functional and dysfunctional aspects of ideology and bureaucracy; obviously, sociological analysis had explored the corresponding paradoxes a long time ago. I hope that our understanding of the mechanisms of individual psychology that feed into and codetermine aggressive conflicts at the social level of interactions may contribute to the understanding, and perhaps even to reducing the destructive impact, of human aggression in our social systems.

120   Otto F. Kernberg

REFERENCES

Anzieu, D. (1984). *The Group and the Unconscious*. London: Routledge & Kegan Paul.

Bion, W. R. (1961). *Experiences in Groups*. New York: Basic Books.

Canetti, E. (1960). *Crowds and Power*. New York: Seabury Press.

Chasseguet-Smirgel, J. (1984). *The Ego Ideal*. New York: W. W. Norton.

Durkheim, E. (1893). *The Division of Labor in Society*. George Simpson, trans. New York: Macmillan. 1933.

———. (1925). *Moral Education: A Study in the Theory and Application of the Sociology of Education*. Everett K. Silson and Herman Schnurer, trans. New York: The Free Press of Glencoe. 1961.

Freud, S. (1921). Group psychology and the analysis of the ego. *S.E.*, 18:65–143.

Jacobson, E. (1971). *Depression*. New York: International Universities Press.

Jacques, E. (1976). *A General Theory of Bureaucracy*. New York: Halsted.

Kernberg, O. F. (1980). *Internal World and External Reality: Object Relations Theory Applied*. New York: Jason Aronson.

———. (1989). The temptations of conventionality. *International Review of Psychoanalysis*, 16:191–205.

———. (1993). Paranoiagenesis in organizations. In *Comprehensive Textbook of Group Psychotherapy*. 3rd ed. H. Kaplan and B. J. Sadock, eds. Baltimore: Williams & Wilkins, pp. 47–57.

———. (1994). Mass psychology through the analytic lens. In *The Spectrum of Psychoanalysis: Essays in Honor of Martin Bergmann*. A. K. Richards and A. D. Richards, eds. Madison, Conn.: International Universities Press, pp. 257–281.

Kolakowski, L. (1978). *Main Currents of Marxism: 3. The Breakdown*. Oxford: Oxford University Press.

Malia, M. (1994). *The Soviet Tragedy*. New York: Free Press.

Masters, R. D. (1989). *The Nature of Politics*. New Haven: Yale University Press.

McCarthy, C. M. (1978). *Report of the Task Force on Regulation on the Cost of Regulation*. Hospital Association of New York State.

Michels, R. (1911). *Political Parties: A Sociological Study of the Oligarchical Tendencies in Modern Democracy*. Eden and Cedar Paul, trans. New York: Free Press. 1949.

Nesbit, R. (1993). *The Sociological Tradition*. New Brunswick, N.J.: Transaction.

Sinyavsky, A. (1988). *Soviet Civilization: A Cultural History*. New York: Arcade.

Tocqueville, A. de. (1835–40). *Democracy in America*. Philips Bradley, ed. New York: Alfred Knopf. 1945.

Tönnies, F. (1887). *Community and Society*. Charles Loomis, trans. and ed. New York: Harper Torchbooks. 1963.

Turquet, P. (1975). Threats to identity in the large group. In *The Large Group: Dynamics and Therapy*. L. Kreeger, ed. London: Constable, pp. 87–144.

Voslensky, M. (1983). *Nomenklatura: The Soviet Ruling Class—An Insider's Report*. New York: Doubleday.

Weber, M. (1904–05). *The Protestant Ethic and the Spirit of Capitalism*. Talcott Parsons, trans. New York: Charles Scribner's Sons. 1958.

Zinoviev, A. (1984). *The Reality of Communism*. New York: Schocken Books.

H. Shmuel Erlich

 7 On Discourse with an Enemy

I must confess that I have undertaken the task of addressing this topic with a great deal of uneasiness. Living in Israel and in the Middle East in these times, and being an Israeli and a Jew, makes the subject of an enemy uncomfortably close; it is a strain on one's objectivity and neutrality. But to deal with this question from the point of view of psychoanalysis and psychoanalytically informed group relations has proved even more difficult than I had anticipated.

The question itself seems fairly straightforward: *enemy* is a ubiquitous designation and perception of our daily life with which we are all familiar. We have learned about the enemies of our nation in school, and we have all had, and still have, our childhood, adolescent, and adult life enemies. Some of us, depending on our age and experience, have known enemies on the battlefield, either firsthand or remotely. Our daily politics are full of old and new enemies, real and imagined ones. We all have a good deal to say about enemies and enmity as well-informed citizens and members of society. But do we, as psychoanalysts, have anything of importance to contribute to the understanding of what an enemy is, or how to deal with him or her? Can psychoanalysis tell us anything that is unique and pertinent about this problem? And does it have any course or solution to offer?

The answers to these questions are not easily forthcoming, nor are they particularly encouraging. The peculiar fact is that until recently psychoanalysis has almost entirely avoided direct engagement with these questions. Freud twice addressed the subject of war (1915, 1932). Much later, attention was focused on war again (Fornari, 1966) and in a symposium held in Israel on the "Psychological Bases of War" (Winnik et al., 1973). Prompted by the threat of the Cold War in the 1980s, the organization of Psychoanalysts for the Prevention of Nuclear War took a practical and political stance on human self-destructiveness and the meaning of silence in the face of such tendencies (Segal, 1987), and an entire issue of *Psychoanalytic Inquiry* was devoted to "Aggression in International Relations" (Mack, 1986). At the same time, Volkan (1985, 1986, 1988) offered a valuable elucidation of the concept of "enemy" to which I shall return. Several attempts in the Israel Psychoanalytic Society to address issues raised by the occupation of the West Bank and the Intifada have frankly failed. The general conclusion was that we were entitled to our own opinions as private citizens, but that our psychoanalytic background did not warrant a claim for a special position in these matters.

This relative dearth of meaningful contributions to the problem of enmity may appear baffling and almost bizarre in view of the central concern of psychoanalysis with conflict and drive, rivalry and competition, envy and greed, sadism and masochism, aggression and hatred, and even death and destructiveness. Is it legitimate, however, to reduce questions about enemy and enmity to these considerations? Do these concepts provide us with all the necessary and sufficient tools for dealing with this essential human phenomenon?

Enemies are usually encountered in the social sphere. The term designates a person or force that is regarded with hostility or believed to harbor hostile intentions toward us. An enemy may also, however, dwell within us; this is indeed one of the aspects highlighted through psychoanalysis. It seems to me that the heart of the difficulty of understanding and dealing with the notion of an enemy and enmity is that it is one of the most powerful, not to say dangerous, emanations of the conjunction of the inner world and the outer world. I propose that, difficult as that may be, we must learn to think of enmity as an entity spanning internal and external reality, the subjective inner world and the objective environment. Enmity is also, however, a bridge between "self" and "otherness," and hence also, at another level, between individual and group phenomena. Talking with an enemy is usually regarded as a significant advance toward resolving conflicts, insofar as it provides an alternative to physical fighting and allows for a symbolic level of discourse. Dialogue with an enemy is often, however, not possible for a long time, and depends on the kind of enemy he or she is perceived to be. A Palestinian leader has recently said: "There are two kinds of enemies: the enemy you talk to, and the enemy you don't talk to." The dramatic handshake of Yitzhak Rabin and Yasser Arafat, viewed across a shrinking world with hope, disbelief, and astonishment by people far removed from the actual conflict, marked the instantaneous transformation of the enemy one does not talk to into an enemy one talks with. What defines the enemy we talk to, or the one we don't talk to? How can we turn an enemy we don't discourse with into one that we do? The answer to these dilemmas seems to me to lie in the dynamics of creativity. It is probably as creative an act as we may ever be able to perform, to be able to regard an enemy as part of us and yet as existing separately and in his or her own right.

I intend to look at enemy and enmity from the perspectives of individual-intrapsychic and group relations dynamics. I shall touch on key concepts like boundary, otherness and strangeness, and large-group processes. My remarks are roughly divided into three areas. First, I shall examine enmity within the psychoanalytic and the group-process frames of reference. Second, I shall focus on certain characteristics and derivatives of these approaches, reviewing different levels of discourse with an enemy. Last, and perhaps most important, I shall touch on the most difficult question: does our examination of this subject point to or offer guidelines for potential solutions?

THE CONCEPT OF AN ENEMY

Psychoanalysis has always had to contend with the tension between an interactive-interpersonal and an internal-subjective perspective. The preference in psychoanalysis, however, has usually been for elucidating and interpreting the intrapsychic realm. The level the theory speaks of is that of internal fields of forces, perhaps best described as internal relationships and relatedness. It has far less to say about real social and political relationships.

What seems to emerge from a review of the intrapsychic level is that we can distinguish between two enemy categories which differ in terms of psychic structure, internal organization, and developmental level. The earlier, more primitive kind is the preoedipal enemy. The relationship with this enemy is governed by splitting and projective identification; it is marked by polarization and uncompromised evil. In Volkan's terms (1986), this enemy is the best suitable target for the externalization of all our bad parts. Ego and superego levels mobilized are earlier and more primitive; they involve concreteness and lack of readiness for symbolic treatment and discourse, and readily tend toward direct expressions of drives and drive derivatives, like oral rage and cannibalistic wishes and fantasies. These levels of relatedness render this an enemy with whom we cannot have a discourse. Talking, or, more correctly, verbal exchange, may occur, but it is in the service of the direct and literal expression and satisfaction of aggressive and destructive wishes and impulses. Words become weapons and are used to attack, invade, dominate, and eviscerate the enemy.

The more sophisticated and advanced enemy is the oedipal enemy, with whom we can have a talking discourse. The internal relatedness to the oedipal enemy is marked by the complexity that characterizes post-ambivalent relationships, with negative feelings of hatred and rivalry, but also with positive feelings of love, admiration, identification, and emulation. The relationship with the oedipal enemy draws on more advanced ego and superego organizations. Defense mechanisms used are also more mature; they involve repression and more sophisticated levels of psychological operations, like symbolization and abstraction. Stern's (1985) description of the "verbal self" as the highest self-organization achieved in early development is relevant here. The higher level signified by verbal development, abstract thought, and symbolization has, however, causes and implications that are inherent to the level of verbal discourse, yet go far beyond the mere fact of verbalization. They suggest a third frame of reference, a shared cultural order and a type of "otherness," on which I shall expand below.

The intrapsychic enemy becomes a realistic enemy when it manifests itself in social reality. The main arena in which this takes place is that of relationships within and between groups. My remarks here are based on Bion's (1961) work in groups and on numerous observations of these processes within Tavistock Group Relations Conferences, which study group processes in the tradition of Bion and others.[1]

One notion that comes out of this work is that of being positioned "on the boundary." This notion needs to be expanded and explicated. Boundaries occupy a central position in psychoanalytic ego-psychology and in systemic models of group and organizational behavior. Boundaries involve notions of strength and permeability as well as rigidity and elasticity. Above all, there is usually some question about the degree of clarity with which they are set up and defined. Boundaries are also, however, meeting grounds where different sides can and do come in contact with one another. Boundaries sometimes allow, or include, a certain amount of "no-man's-land" which is not clearly under the jurisdiction of any party. Often enough such no-man's-land is precisely the territory in which encounters and testing of limits take place without the danger and

1. This working model, and its theoretical underpinnings and developments, are described in Colman and Bexton (1975) and Colman and Geller (1985).

risk of all-out war with full responsibility and consequences. In psycho-analytic terms, this suggests the transitional space and transitional phenomena described by Winnicott (1971). I have pointed out that boundaries may be drawn sharply between self and object, contributing to their definition and separateness; they may also, however, encircle and envelop self and object, as in states of merger and fusion. I have described these differing deployments of boundaries in relation to underlying dimensions of experiencing self and object as Doing or as Being (Erlich, 1990, 1993).

It is extremely helpful to think of boundaries not as well-defined, razor thin lines, which cannot support or contain any life, but as gray areas and no-man's territories, in which a great deal of actual and significant living takes place. This usually happens through some variety of "play"—in the sense that it does not lead immediately to real consequences in well-defined areas of living. The concept of a moratorium is an important instance of such playful extension of boundaries, in this case of temporal and role boundaries, in the transition from late adolescence to adulthood.

Such a boundary region, or better yet frontier zone, has much to offer in terms of elasticity and permeability. Very often, it can give birth to and support what is creative, novel, and psychologically pertinent. Not only positive creative aspects of life, however, have their roots here; negative creations, such as enmity, are also fundamentally linked to the psychological transactions and creations at the boundary. It is this domain and the kind of life that exists within and close to it that I have in mind when I speak of the enemy as created and coming to life on the boundary.

If we consider for a moment the dynamics that take place in a large group, we find that enmity occupies a pivotal role. A perennial and centrally important maneuver in the large group is to designate an enemy. One way this takes place is by splitting the large group into subgroups and splinter-systems. Such fragmenting of the whole seems so natural, and occurs so frequently and swiftly, that it is difficult to discern and track. This process of divisiveness is the equivalent of the intrapsychic splitting of the whole bad object in order to assimilate and subjugate it.

The governing fantasy is to reduce the intolerable tension by bringing about "peace"—that wished-for state in which the ongoing and difficult frustration will finally stop—through one subgroup gaining control over the entire group. The actual struggles produced by this elusive fantasy-wish can lead to extremely destructive behavior, ranging from the stark violence of the lynch mob to the fragmentation and disappearance of clear thinking and adaptive reality testing in academic large-group settings. Behind the multiple splits and fights against a shifting variety of enemies is, however, the unconscious wish for final and total submersion in the whole, for a state in which the individual will cease to be a problem because of his or her separate existence and identity. To hold on to one's identity and individuality in the large group may therefore be tantamount to an act of war and should not be undertaken without sufficient strength to back it up, for the counterattack will not fail to come. The group feels threatened by individuality and individuation, which hinders its quest for peace through homogeneity. It will mobilize its destructiveness in order to diffuse this dangerous and offensive individuality and submerge it in the totality of the large group. Threats to identity in the large group (Turquet, 1975) thus come from two sides: one source is the wish to submerge oneself in the totality of the group, leading to the acquiescent, willing undermining and erosion of one's personal identity; the other source is the actual aggressive threat of the large group against its internal enemy—one's claim to adhere to and develop one's personal identity within it.

Enmity within the large group is thus a tremendously fluctuating, treacherous, and diffuse entity. An enemy identified one moment may be totally disregarded the next. Under these conditions, it is impossible to carry on meaningful discourse with either friend or foe. It is this constant internal shifting and fluidity that makes the large group so dangerous. Its internal instability allows it to be tilted suddenly and irrationally in the direction in which an enemy is identified. The discovery of an external enemy brings about a momentary stabilization of the group, and hence an alleviation of its tremendous inner tensions. This makes the large group extremely vulnerable to being manipulated into seeking and destroying real or imaginary enemies. Once again, the enemy takes shape on the group's boundary, be it a physical, geographical, or ideological boundary. In this boundary region of the large group we find many different sorts of enemies: barbarian invaders, religious heretics, false messiahs, and political reformers bent on changing the group. As leadership is always a boundary function, the group's own leaders are also on the boundary and may easily and momentarily be turned into its enemies. History is full of accounts that substantiate this thesis; recent events in Eastern Europe offer a number of pertinent examples.

HOW DOES ONE HAVE DISCOURSE WITH AN ENEMY?

There seem to be several stock alternatives or preferred answers to this question. The one most idealized in our age is that of talking to an enemy. A caricatured version of this appeared in the 1967 movie *Cool Hand Luke*, where the catch phrase of the Bad Guy was, "What we've got here is a failure to communicate." This drawled-out declaration preceded the institution of some form of maddening cruelty. Freud's preferred solution discloses his powerful rationalistic bias. While war is regarded as stemming from instinctual drives, discourse with the enemy originates in the rational and reality-bound part of man, in the service of adaptation and survival (Freud, 1915b). Freud's leanings toward rationalistic conflict resolution were deeply embedded in the cultural and ideological tradition in which he grew up (Gay, 1988) and which he continued to represent almost in spite of himself. A straight line leads from this rationalistic bias to the pessimism he expressed on many occasions.

Other schools of psychoanalysis, particularly the Kleinian, offer the solution of splitting off the bad and threatening aspects of oneself and projecting them into the object. This allows for maintaining simultaneous distance from and relatedness to the object by means of projective identification, in which the object is both preserved and controlled (Segal, 1964). Splitting off the threatening, anxiety-producing parts of oneself alleviates the anxiety that threatens the ego with disintegration. Similarly, projecting valued parts of the self into an idealized good object serves as a defense against impending loss and separation. Projecting these split-off parts into the external object and identifying it with them mean that they now control and possess the object. In this way the object is experienced as under the control of parts of the self that are now "encapsulated" in it (Bion, 1962). The object is thus related to in a manner that preserves and controls it, as a source of either idealized or threatening parts of the self, depending on the nature of what was projected into it. This defensive process actually implies efforts to relate to the object through its infiltration, conquest, splitting, and dissolution, with the eventual result being its absorption and assimilation into the self. These are not efforts at speaking or having a dialogue with the enemy, but of controlling and dominating him by penetrating and intruding into him (projective identification), or by mastering him through his becoming a part of the self (introjective identification) (Bion, 1962). This is also tantamount to cannibalizing the enemy and, at a higher level, absorbing him through intermarriage and cultural assimilation.

Assimilation of the enemy at a more advanced level takes place through identification with the aggressor. In this defensive mode, fear of the menacing figure is handled through its internalization and identification with it at the expense of the self. The child identifying with the aggressor experiences himself as possessing the latter's power and might. He can now act, and indeed he does, as he experiences this aggressor. He adopts patterns of thought, values, and behavior that characterize his object of identification, not himself. This mechanism is widespread (in connection with surviving the Holocaust, as well as Chinese and Japanese treatment of prisoners of war) and evermore dangerous. While positive identification out of love and appreciation is rewarded by the enrichment of the self, identification with the aggressor out of fear exacts a heavy price in terms of the alienation and shrinking of the self and setting up a false self-organization (Thompson, 1940; Winnicott, 1960). In extreme cases this mechanism may lead to a degree of impoverishment of the self that reaches borderline and even psychotic proportions.

Identification with the aggressor points to the dangers of appeasement, of dealing with the enemy in an acquiescent, nonconfrontational, noncombative way. As morally distasteful and potentially dangerous as it may be to respond forcefully to aggression, there is also danger in not fighting back, in yielding and assimilating one's own identity with that of the enemy. Such a course may clearly lead to one's disappearance as a viable psychological and/or physical entity. This eventuality must therefore always be weighed against the quest for preserving peace at any cost.

So far we have discussed the enemy who is familiar and so close as to be part of the self. The enemy is, however, also the "other" who is unfamiliar and unknown. It is in this sense that he (the enemy may, of course, be male or female) appears at the specific developmental stage of around eight months of age, and his very appearance—always experienced as surprising and unexpected—arouses existential fright and anxiety. This "other-stranger" who provokes this stranger-anxiety is frightening because of his very otherness. He appears at the exact moment when fusion with the mother becomes an almost conscious source of pleasure and security, stemming from the experience of blissful merger. The stranger threatens to undercut and interrupt that merger. This usually provokes in the infant an immediate focusing of attention, reorganization, mobilization of forces, and readiness to face danger—in brief, an arousal and anxiety response. The extent to which the arousal gives rise to curiosity and exploration—as against anxiety, apprehension, and projection—is probably co-determined by a number of factors. It may well be related to the mother-child dyadic capacity for establishing and tolerating transitional space and phenomena. This capacity, in turn, may have to do with the extent to which dyadic interaction is characterized by a "goodness of fit," in which both parties are capable of affective attunement (Stern, 1985) and synchronization of their experiential modalities (Erlich and Blatt, 1985). The extent to which the stranger's appearance arouses anxiety is especially related to the degree of dyadically experienced security about Being-relatedness (Erlich, 1990), i.e., the experience of merger and union. Where this is shaky, the infant is more prone to mobilize into a Doing-mode, in which preparatory anxiety responses are augmented.

The anxiety response to the stranger is universal. Enlarging on this, we may say that the stranger is the prototype of the internal psychic enemy that becomes a social reality. His threat is the very archaic threat to destroy our peace, to snatch us out of the calmness that comes through Being—the merger with another in the experience of simply being alive. Historically and currently, there is always great readiness to project onto the stranger this role of the enemy, the "destroyer of the peace." But who is this stranger? The stranger I am talking about is not a distant and unknown entity. He lives close by, almost within society, yet is not fully a part of it. He occupies a "boundary position," like the leader in the group and the analyst in the psychoanalytic situation. Taking up the boundary position makes all of them natural targets for the projection of hatred and enmity. We see here the confluence of the enemy as a boundary creature and the other-stranger as both a stimulator and an object of enmity.

Such fence-straddling otherness, close and familiar and yet also different and strange, was depicted by Volkan (1986) as "the best reservoir for our bad externalized parts . . . [so that they] would be located in things and people who resemble us or are at least familiar to us—such as neighbors" (p. 187). At the same time, however, since "we do not wish to acknowledge on a conscious level that the enemy is like us," there sets in "the narcissism of minor difference" (ibid.)—a ritualistic focus on and enlargement of minor signs and distinctions in order to help differentiate between oneself and the "enemy-other."

This dual role of the other-stranger also plays an important part in the course of development, where stranger-anxiety gradually turns into recognition of the other's separate and independent existence. This recognition is an important basis for the development and maintenance of mature object relations (Sandler, 1977). It has, however, an additional facet. The anxiety in the face of the stranger-enemy is a primary, almost reflexive reminder of the limitations and liabilities of the self. In this sense it provides a necessary condition for realistic self-definition. Paradoxically, then, the anxiety stirred up in relation to the stranger-enemy provides a catalyst for the process of self-definition. To paraphrase, if there were no enemy, we would have had to invent him.

ARE THERE ANY SOLUTIONS?

Is it possible to find ways of talking and communicating with an enemy? I should like to finish with an attempt, almost certainly frustratingly partial and insufficient, to draw some tentative conclusions from what has been surveyed so far.

After analyzing the wish of nations to obtain their interests and passions, in his "Thoughts for the Times on War and Death," Freud (1915) poses the following dilemma: "It is, to be sure, a mystery why the *collective individuals* should in fact despise, hate and detest one another—every nation against every other—and even in times of peace. I cannot tell why that is so. It is just as though *when it becomes a question of a number of people*, not to say millions, all individual moral acquisitions are obliterated, and only the most primitive, the oldest, the crudest mental attitudes are left" (p. 288; italics mine). Freud finishes on a sober note, with an appeal for greater honesty and openness in relationships among people, and mainly with the authorities, which he expects will lead toward a turning point.

I believe that this hope is no longer so simplistically held and shared by all of us. It has been the bitter lesson of this century to come to distrust authority and to come to know its irrational and dangerous sides. Indeed, even the psychoanalytic establishment has not escaped criticism for its monolithic stance and what is perceived as the authoritarian nature of its inner political structure.

Freud feels that it is the individual who can be approached and understood, while it is the group, and particularly the large group, that makes human behavior so primitive and irrational. Some advances have taken place in our understanding since Freud's lines were written at the time of the First World War. I suggest that enmity is indeed an inherent part of the individual human psyche; but enmity is also on the boundary between internal and external reality. It takes on its familiar meaning and shape as a social phenomenon when we meet and work with it at the group, system, and organizational levels. These levels, therefore, can no longer be ignored by psychoanalytic thinking.

This brings us back briefly to the dynamics of the large group. From all we know about these processes, even under the relatively controlled conditions of a working conference and with the participation of consultants, there can be only one conclusion: Large-group processes, with their fluctuations, regressions, and fragmentations, are highly lawful and regular. This is so even when the participants have had the benefit of previous experience and impressive educational and cultural achievements. Therefore, if our aim is rational, enlightened political activity, large-group settings and events must be avoided and prevented as much as possible. It has been recently demonstrated again that large masses of people can be instrumental in changing the political order. But it is equally true that such mass movements and revolutionary upheavals may go in many directions; they do not always lead to freedom and democracy. There were large crowds and mobs involved in so many revolutions—in France, Russia, Nazi Germany, China, and more recently in Eastern Europe. The phenomenon of mass uprising is intertwined with popular visions of democracy; it provides, however, no assurances of the eventual outcome nor any protection against the danger of being manipulated by sinister powers to their own ends. Wherever possible, and especially where negotiations take place, small groups should be preferred to large groups. This may well be true also for gatherings that are not manifestly (yet are implicitly) political, such as symposia and conventions. Negotiations between enemy parties to a conflict need not only the small-group format, however. They also require the clarity and firmness of boundaries that guard against premature exposure, which threatens to throw the process back into the large group.

The small-group format in itself is, however, no guarantee for dialogue. Indeed, the need for dialogue is often glibly and unthinkingly advanced. Our own professional and personal biases (I am speaking as a psychoanalyst) are intertwined here in ways that may produce complications or even fallacies. We are trained in dialogue, and our deep belief in and commitment to discourse and discussion may sometimes border on a magical belief in the power of words. We tend to forget the tremendous importance of the psychoanalytic setting, with its combination of strict boundaries and open-endedness, in enabling, shaping, and contributing to the creation of dialogue, and then only after expending much time and tremendous efforts. Having witnessed attempts at dialogue with "labeled enemies" in professional group settings, I have been amazed at the degree and speed with which such sessions can become confrontational and coercive. Dialogue is based on the ability to recognize and respect the other's essential and rightful difference; this is diametrically opposed to regarding him or her as an enemy. We may be able to extend ourselves and even accord dialogic consideration to an opponent or an adversary. It is much more difficult to do this with a declared enemy, whose very designation as such immediately places him or her beyond the dialogic pale.

These dialogic considerations are related to the differentiation made above between preoedipal and oedipal enemies. The distinction between these two enemies was seen to be a function of the developmental levels at which they are encountered, whether the encounter is primary and takes place in childhood, or a later, adult-life derivative. These differences account for an enemy with whom we can and do have discourse, as against one with whom we cannot and do not. A closer look into this differentiation reveals, however, that the different levels at which we experience our oedipal enemy are not confined to the mere verbality of the exchange, but extends to the wider implications and connotations of words and symbols.

Symbol formation is often approached from the vantage point of either the intrapsychic, emotional, and cognitive development that enables it, or the extra-individual, cultural framework that contains and transmits these symbols as cultural artifacts and into which the individual is induced. The area in which cultural symbols are created and used is, however, better conceived as a "third" area, which is, in Winnicott's (1971) sense, the area of shared experience that gives rise to play and creativity. This third area, which is indeed where culture comes into being, is the transitional space that envelops the mother-child dyad just as it is being created by them. Situated between the inner world and the external one, between subjective objects and realities and objective ones, it provides an experiential bridge that allows both sides to become alive, to be experienced as psychologically real and viable. This is also, however, the juncture where the oedipal constellation comes together with the notion of transitional space: both are founded on experience, recognition, and encounter with a "third" entity. Oedipal development requires, above all else, the capacity for recognition of a third, an other whose existence is on the boundary of the earlier established dyadic oneness and mutuality. Recognition of the other-stranger can be the source of anxiety and apprehension, in which the stranger is the enemy. If, however, the other, or the "third," is experienced as being created and coming to life on this boundary, occupying a space and sharing a frame that partakes of the communality of the dyad, he will be related to positively, as an object of curiosity and exploration.

How does this come about? It seems that the dyadically created transitional space is able to accommodate a "third," which is experienced as an intrinsic part of it, when he or she shares and participates in the framework that enables the transitional space in the first place—a frame of creative illusion and shared symbols. The accommodation of the "third" is therefore greatly assisted and transacted by symbols of various kinds. Symbols, by their very nature, are experienced as such a "third"—a semiotic frame that is neither entirely of the self, nor of the mother-environment, but that exists both separately and yet together with the united and merged self-object dyad. Thus symbols—words and language, sounds and gestures, bodily expressions and cultural artifacts—are all part of the wider framework we call culture, of a "third world," encompassing self and other and lending experience its special form, content, and means for further developmental transmutation. It is in this sense that we can have discourse with an oedipal enemy: We share with him not merely a language, but the comforting and enabling experience of the shared frame created out of common language and cultural symbols. Although to the observer this may appear to be a discourse between two sides, in actuality it takes place between two who are aware of their common "third leg"—the wider framework they share and adhere to, and even invest with authority. We may thus claim that oedipal experience has its roots in much earlier developmental periods, in which the "third," or other, though not yet a real partner, nevertheless exists as a potential presence on the boundary of shared experience, where such potential transitional phenomena are created. Preoedipal development, in this sense, refers to an absence of or disability in having this creative experience, and being doomed to a mere "two-person" existence, and therefore to splitting and projection, and to having enemies with whom one cannot share anything, let alone have a discourse.

The actual importance of the third in preventing movement toward splitting may be observed in small groups, where the presence of a consultant who takes up the role of such a third contributes significantly to the management of projections that lead to breakdown of discourse. The centrality of the role of the third in political negotiations between enemy parties—transforming preoedipal, nontalking enemies into oedipal enemies capable of discourse—is vividly illustrated by the part played by the United States in the peace talks between Israel and its Arab neighbors, which reaches far beyond that of an arbiter or courier. It is striking that in all of the White House peace ceremonies, beginning with the Camp David Accords and down to the latest declarations of peace with the PLO and Jordan, the pictorial image is always a triadic one, in which the presence of the president of the United States provides the significant third side of the triangle that enables the Israeli and Arab leaders to shake hands.

It is unrealistic to make prescriptions for advancing societies from one developmental level to another. Such complex movement takes place and is measurable only over protracted historical time units. One wonders, however, whether in the shrinking universal village of our times changes may be induced that might contribute to the creation of common, cross-cultural semiotic and symbolic frames of reference, which could in turn foster a sense of shared actual frames of reference. The development of common languages, symbolic systems, and cultural heritage can contribute much to the alleviation of unresolved enmities. Modern technology and communication media have already gone a long way toward creating certain collective cultural vistas. Perhaps more could be done. However, this is in no way a utopian dream of messianic peace and millennium. It is merely a step, of limited potential, toward turning preoedipal into oedipal enemies. If it is true, as Volkan says, that "our current knowledge of human nature tells us that enemies are here to stay" (1986, p. 190), then perhaps the best we can hope for is to change the enemy from his preoedipal position of total badness and evil to the oedipal level of rivalry and competitiveness coupled with love and affection, and thus from the enemy to whom we do not talk to the enemy with whom we can and do talk.

The current peace talks between Israel and the Arabs provide an example of how actual contact contributes to the reduction of strangeness and projections. Yet contact will probably produce new and unforeseen difficulties and in itself is no guarantee of the disappearance of enmity and the triumph of reason and peace. Many other factors interact with and activate the psychological ones. Siblings who become enemies over dividing an inheritance are not strangers, but the loss suddenly revives old anxieties of shortage, lack of supplies, and fantasies that there may not be enough for all. We must be open to the entire range of realistic possibilities, including the emergence of new and insurmountable difficulties, as relationships with yesterday's enemies develop and deepen.

It seems that the understanding of the concept of enemy presents us with numerous paradoxes. An enemy at one and the same time partakes of so many opposites: internal and external reality, preoedipal and oedipal, other-stranger and known-familiar, a part of us and yet not. These seeming contradictions and paradoxes lead to the understanding I suggested here, namely that "enemy" is a boundary concept, or a transitional entity, which occupies an exceedingly important intrapsychic position and social role where so many human attributes and dilemmas come together, where so many polar dimensions and entities actually meet. To understand what an enemy is, is to understand what is essentially human.

In closing, let me address once again the issue of distance and lack of it in our relatedness to the enemy. As Volkan (1986) has noted, the enemy tends to be our neighbor, who is closer and more similar to us than we care to admit, leading to narcissistic highlighting of minor differences in the service of differentiating ourselves from him. His closeness and similarity make the neighbor, however, a suitable target for externalization and projection of the "bad" parts of ourselves in the first place. Our ability to have discourse with an enemy is therefore related to the degree to which he can be defined clearly and is not too closely intertwined with our own self-definition. Distance, boundaries, and separateness make the task of discourse more manageable, though not necessarily more creative. Splitting, projective identification, identification with the aggressor, and similar regression-enhancing conditions make differentiation and individuation of ourselves and the enemy more difficult, rendering talking and discourse impossible. Perceiving the enemy as the preoedipal "other" leads to his dehumanization and demonization. A more advanced, oedipal view of the enemy's "otherness," however, enhances the discourse. At the triangular-oedipal level of development, acceptance of the enemy's "otherness" is a concession to his humanness, to his being a part and a member of the same widely shared entity—the "third" presence of human cultural existence. Such communality, however, also paradoxically allows for the differentiation and individuation of persons and groups; it alone can ensure creative conflict resolution instead of fighting and destruction. Under suitable psychological and developmental conditions, "otherness" can provide a basis for novel and creative contact and intercourse replacing relatedness through fantasy alone, which can foster the wish to destroy and assimilate the enemy.

Truly creative discourse with the enemy can come only with our willingness to immerse ourselves in the "potential space" we both share, in which parts of the enemy and parts of ourselves are fused and intermingled. We may then be able to perceive, however briefly and fleetingly, the shared elements of our common humanity. One of the most creative acts we may ever be capable of is experiencing our enemy as a part of ourselves, while also recognizing his existence in his own right, as separate and distinct from us.

REFERENCES

Bion, W. R. (1961). *Experiences in Groups*. London: Tavistock.
———. (1962). *Learning from Experience*. London: Heinemann.
Colman, A. D., and Bexton, W. H. (1975). *Group Relations Reader*. Grex, Calif.: A. K. Rice Institute Series.
Colman, A. D., and Geller, M. H. (1985). *Group Relations Reader 2*. Washington, D.C.: A. K. Rice Institute.
Erlich, H. S. (1990). Boundaries, limitations, and the wish for fusion in the treatment of adolescents. *Psychoanalytic Study of the Child*, 45:195–213.
———. (1993). Reality, fantasy, and adolescence. *Psychoanalytic Study of the Child*, 48:209–223.
Erlich, H. S., and Blatt, S. J. (1985). Narcissism and object love. *Psychoanalytic Study of the Child*, 40:57–79.
Fornari, F. (1966). *The Psychoanalysis of War*. Bloomington: Indiana University Press (1975).
Freud, S. (1915). Thoughts for the times on war and death. *Standard Edition*, 14:273–302.
———. (1932). Why war? *Standard Edition*, 22:197–215.
Gay, P. (1988). *Freud: A Life for Our Time*. New York: W. W. Norton.
Mack, J. E. (1986). Aggression and its alternatives in the conduct of international relations. *Psychoanalytic Inquiry*, 6:135–314.
Sandler, A.-M. (1977). Beyond eight-months anxiety. *International Journal of Psycho-analysis*, 58:195–207.
Segal, H. (1964). *Introduction to the Work of Melanie Klein*. London: Heinemann.
———. (1987). Silence is the real crime. *International Journal of Psycho-analysis*, 14:3–12.
Stern, D. N. (1985). *The Interpersonal World of the Infant*. New York: Basic Books.
Thompson, C. (1940). Identification with the enemy and loss of the sense of self. *Psychoanalytic Quarterly*, 9:37–50.
Turquet, P. M. (1975). Threats to identity in the large group. In *The Large Group: Dynamics and Therapy*, L. Kreeger, ed. London: Constable.
Volkan, V. D. (1985). The need to have enemies and allies: A developmental approach. *Political Psychology*, 6:219–247.
———. (1986). The narcissism of minor differences in the psychological gap between opposing nations. *Psychoanalytic Inquiry*, 6:175–191.

———. (1988). *The Need to Have Enemies and Allies*. Northvale, N.J.: Jason Aronson.

Winnicott, D. W. (1960). Ego distortion in terms of true and false self. In *The Maturational Processes and the Facilitating Environment*. London: Hogarth Press (1979).

———. (1971). *Playing and Reality*. London: Tavistock.

Winnik, H. Z., Moses, R., and Ostow, M. (1973). *Psychological Bases of War*. New York: Quadrangle Books.

Carol Gilligan

It behooves you to go by another way . . .
If you would escape from this wild place.
—Dante, *Inferno*

◼ 8 Remembering Iphigenia: Voice, Resonance, and the Talking Cure

VOICE AND RESONANCE: THE INNER WORLD IN THE OUTER WORLD

Eleven-year-old Nina tells me that she is writing a story about "someone during the Civil War" and making her story "a little bit sad," because when the father goes to war, the girl is "really upset." Nina says, "He talks to her before he goes, about how he feels about leaving and that he is just as worried as she is, or more worried and more scared. . . . And, you know, she feels like he's never going to come back, which is possible, but, you know, it's not a fact yet. So she has a very, um, a very strange feeling sometimes." I ask Nina about this strange feeling, and she explains, "Before he left, she realized that he was not, um, totally powerful, but she didn't, um, feel angry at him for that, but she felt very, um, very sorry, sort

of very sorry for him, and very shocked or surprised, mainly, and still upset that he was leaving. And, um, he was trying to comfort her when he
told her about, um, about his own fears of going, but really she was just
mainly surprised, and she hadn't realized that he could feel like this too."

I have known Nina for almost a year at the time of this interview conversation. A gifted writer, she is taking part in a study of girls' development and a prevention project designed to strengthen girls' voices and
their courage (see Gilligan, Rogers, and Noel, 1992; Gilligan and
Rogers, 1993).[1] I ask Nina why the girl in the story didn't know "that her
father could feel like this too," and she continues her layered and psychologically nuanced description of the girl, the father, and the flow of
realizations and feelings between them: "He had always been there for
her, you know. She had been, um, she'd been hurt . . . and she had been
humiliated because she was a girl. And he always understood her, and she
was very close to him. Her siblings thought it was really brave of him to
[enlist] right away, but she knew that he was, he just, if he waited any
longer he wouldn't be able to do it, he wouldn't have enough courage to
do it." How did she know that? "She knew because of the way he talked
to her, that he was feeling really scared and upset, and he didn't want her
to make it any harder or anything. After that, she didn't get so upset, or,
she didn't show it." By listening to "the way he talked to her," the girl
picks up her father's fear and his upset feelings, and also his need to cover
these feelings in order to enlist in the army. Sensing his vulnerability and

1. Nina was one of eighteen girls who took part in a three-year study of girls'
development and a prevention project involving the creation of Theater, Writing, and Outing Clubs designed to strengthen girls' voices, girls' courage, and relationships between girls and women. The girls came from families that differed
racially, culturally, by social class and family composition. Ten girls attended an
urban public school; eight girls, including Nina, were students at an experimental, coeducational independent elementary school at the time the project began.
Three women were involved in the project: Dr. Annie Rogers, a clinical and developmental psychologist and a poet; Normi Noel, a theater director, actor, voice
teacher, and writer; and myself. For a complete report of the project see Gilligan
and Rogers (1993).

also his wish that she not make it any harder for him, she also covers her feelings and begins not to feel so upset or at least not to show how upset she is feeling.

The following year when Nina is twelve and we resume our interview conversation, she tells me again of the stories she is writing—-stories that are winning prizes in local contests. But now the inner world of the Civil War story is nowhere in evidence. In contrast to her intimate and direct, naturalistic rendering of the human world, Nina writes about how "things would feel" if they "were able to see, like a pen with its cap off." In one story, a girl "is trying to, well, she falls in love with this boy . . . and they have these adventures. It starts when they're at a dance, and then when she has to leave, his car gets stolen, and then they go to the gang. . . . This group has stolen it . . . and he has to fight one of the guys, and then they set off in the car, and there's a storm and the car stalls." Nina says, "It's a really good story. I can tell. It's a lot better than the ones I wrote a couple of years ago anyway." In another story, a queen who is "really a bad queen" is assassinated on the anniversary of her coronation. Three generations later, she becomes "a beautiful, wonderful queen." Sensing with me that something is missing—some understanding or even interest in the process of this transformation—Nina observes by way of explanation, "It's just the way memory covers up the bad things." Attributing the cover-up to an "it"—to memory—Nina signals the onset of dissociation.

An inner world has been sequestered, perhaps as the Civil War story suggests, because voicing that world set off disturbing resonances and emotional vibrations in other people, making it harder for them to live in the outer world. Nina has become aware of the difficulties and dangers of being able to feel and to see, or showing what she is seeing and feeling. She also feels the stirring of new desires: to fall in love, to go on romantic adventures, to win prizes in writing contests, to be good and beautiful rather than bad. As the outer world of civilization dims the inner psychological world, casting a shadow over its illumination, Nina for the moment sees this eclipse as the good covering over the bad.

In a short story called "An Unwritten Novel," Virginia Woolf addresses a buried self. The narrator asks, "When the self speaks to the self, who is speaking?" The answer is, "the entombed soul, the spirit driven in, in, in to the central catacomb; the self that took the veil and left the world—a coward perhaps, yet somehow beautiful as it flits with its lantern restlessly up and down the dark corridors" (Woolf, 1921/1982, p. 24). Like Nina at twelve, the writer of Woolf's "unwritten novel" is keeping her light under cover.

In Edith Wharton's short story "The Fullness of Life," the narrator muses: "I have sometimes thought that a woman's nature is like a great house, full of rooms. There is the hall through which everyone passes going in and out. The drawing room where one receives more formal visits, the sitting room where members of the family come and go as they list; but beyond that, far beyond, are other rooms the handles of whose doors are never turned; no one knows the way to them, no one knows whither they lead, and in the innermost room, the holy of holies, the soul sits alone waiting for a footstep that never comes" (Wharton, quoted in Wolff, 1977, pp. 64–65).

This startling, piercing rendition of what the narrator refers to as "a woman's nature" is shocking in part because through the extended simile comparing a woman's nature to a great house, Wharton has so seamlessly joined nature and culture, women and civilization. It is within the great house of civilization that a woman seeks sanctuary in an innermost room, within her own nature, because her soul, unnoticed in both formal and familial relationships, arouses no interest or curiosity. While the soul sits alone silently listening, nobody comes, no one has followed her.

Wharton finds the voice of this early story troubling. Writing to her editor, she explains her wish not to include it in her first published collection: "As to the old short stories of which you speak so kindly, I regard them as the excesses of youth. They were all written 'at the top of my voice.' . . . I may not write any better, but at least I hope that I write in a lower key, and I fear that the voice of those early tales will drown all the others. It is for that reason that I prefer not to publish them" (Wharton, quoted in Wolff, 1977, pp. 63–64). "The Fullness of Life," she says, "is one long shriek."

But this is an old story—this change in voice that signals the suppres-

sion of a brilliant young woman. Picked up by research on girls' development, recorded by women writers in the twentieth century, it was dra-
matized in antiquity by Euripides in his portrayal of Iphigenia.

REMEMBERING IPHIGENIA

When Agamemnon's ships are becalmed at Aulis, he is under internal and external pressure to sacrifice his daughter Iphigenia to the
goddess Artemis in order to gain the winds that will carry his army to
Troy. He writes to Clytemnestra, his wife, telling her to bring Iphigenia
to Aulis, ostensibly for marriage to Achilles. When Iphigenia discovers
her father's purpose, her first response is to say he is mad. He has forgotten their relationship, their closeness, the words they said to one another, their love. It is as if he has forgotten himself. Wishing that she had
the voice of Orpheus so that she could "charm with song the stones to
leap and follow me," or words that could beguile others and work magic,
she says, "O my father," appealing to their relationship and reminding
him,

> I was the first to call you father,
> You to call me child. And of your children
> First to sit upon your knees. We kissed
> Each other in our love. "O Child,"
> You said, "surely one day I shall see you
> Happy in your husband's home. And like
> A flower blooming for me and in my honor."
> Then as I clung to you and wove my fingers
> In your beard, I answered, "Father, you,
> Old and reverent then, with love I shall
> Receive into my home, and so repay you
> For the years of trouble and your fostering
> Care of me." I have in memory all these words
> Of yours and mine. But you, forgetting,
> Have willed it in your heart to kill me.
> . . . .
> Let me win life

> From you. I must. To look upon the world
> Of light is for all men their greatest joy—
> The shadow world below is nothing.
> Men are mad, I say, who pray for death;
> It is better that we live ever so
> Miserably than die in glory.
>   (Euripides, 405 B.C.E./1958, pp. 359–361)

But Agamemnon is caught in a tragic conflict ("Terrible it is to me, my wife, to dare / This thing. Terrible not to dare it"). In the end he feels compelled to sacrifice Iphigenia; "My compulsion [is] absolute," he explains, it is "beyond all will / Of mine" (p. 361).

When Iphigenia takes in the hopelessness of her situation, she chooses to die nobly rather than ignobly, to align herself with her father's purpose, to separate herself from her mother's grief and anger, to "fix [her] mind." She pleads then with Clytemnestra not to make it any harder for her, but instead to "listen to my words," to "hear me now," to "follow my words and tell me if I speak well," to take in how her death can become not a cause for anger but a good and right thing.

> Mother, now listen to my words. I see
> Your soul in anger against your husband.
> This is a foolish and an evil rage.
> Oh, I know when we stand before a helpless
> Doom how hard it is to bear.
> But hear me now.
> . . . .
> And now hear me, Mother,
> What thing has seized me and I have conceived
> In my heart.
> I shall die—I am resolved—
> And having fixed my mind I want to die
> Well and gloriously, putting away
> From me whatever is weak and ignoble.
> Come close to me, Mother, follow my words
> And tell me if I speak well. All Greece turns
> Her eyes to me, to me only, great Greece
> In her might—for through me is the sailing

Of the fleet, through me the sack and overthrow
Of Troy. Because of me, never more will
Barbarians wrong and ravish Greek women,
Drag them from happiness and their homes
In Hellas. The penalty will be paid
Fully for the shame and seizure of Helen.
    And all
These things, all of them, my death will achieve
And accomplish. I, savior of Greece,
Will win honor and my name shall be blessed.
It is wrong for me to love life too deeply. . . .
To Greece I give this body of mine.
Slay it in sacrifice and conquer Troy.
These things coming to pass, Mother, will be
My children, my marriage; through the years
My good name and my glory. It is
A right thing that Greeks rule barbarians,
Not barbarians Greeks. (pp. 369–371)

The chorus, composed of women from the neighboring town of Chalcis, praise Iphigenia's ability to weave what have become corrupt words (love, marriage, conception, children—now linked not with life but with death) into a speech of great dignity: "Child, you play your part with nobleness. / The fault is with the goddess and with fate" (p. 371). Locating the fault with Artemis and with fate, the women of the chorus echo Iphigenia's feelings of helplessness and powerlessness. Initially, the chorus doubled the voice of Clytemnestra, amplifying her plea into the plea of "all women" ("Oh, what a power is motherhood, possessing / A potent spell. All women alike / Fight fiercely for a child" [p. 346]). They urged Agamemnon to "yield to her!" and "save the child," saying, "It is good / That you together save the child. No man / Can rightly speak against this word of mine" (p. 359).

The chorus's turn then signifies the women's internalization of the shame ethic of the culture of honor which both the men and the women are now enforcing, with the stark exception of Clytemnestra. The desire for life and for love has become shameful, and pride has become the overriding motivation (see J. Gilligan, 1996). Iphigenia makes this change explicit when she says, "My good name and my glory" will be "my children, my marriage." And, following Iphigenia, the chorus names her choices of death and victory over a culturally defined dishonor not as madness but as nobility.

The inner and outer worlds are incompatible, and Iphigenia's turn is radical. Her two speeches—the first, an appeal to relationship that proves ineffective, and the second, a wish to go down in history, to be her father's sacrifice and realize as her own his purpose—define a pattern that young women will repeat across the millennia, conveying the powerful suggestion that the father's sacrifice of his adolescent daughter is woven into the fabric of civilization.

In a startling production entitled *Les Atrides*, Ariane Mnouchkine, the creator of the Théâtre du Soleil in Paris, prefaces Aeschylus's *Oresteia* trilogy with Euripides's *Iphigenia in Aulis*, and by doing so radically reframes both the story of the house of Atreus and the birth of Athenian civilization.[2] The *Oresteia*, or story of Orestes, begins with Clytemnestra's murder of Agamemnon as he returns triumphantly from Troy. Orestes, their son, then avenges the murder of his father by killing his mother, and he in turn is pursued by the Furies, until Athena comes and organizes a trial. Bringing the family feud into the public space of the city, she replaces private vengeance with the rule of law and the principle of justice. The *Oresteia*, in dramatizing the long working through of the tensions between the claims of the city and the ties of the household, has long been regarded as the foundational drama of Western civilization. As such, it links the birth of the legal system, the establishment of government or the state, and the origin or hegemony of patriarchy to the freeing of Orestes from the Furies. He is released when Athena casts the deciding vote in his favor at the trial.

By insisting that we remember Iphigenia and hear her story before we listen to the saga of Orestes, by beginning with Agamemnon's sacrifice

2. Ariane Mnouchkine's *Les Atrides* was performed in New York at the Brooklyn Academy of Music in September 1992, and in Paris at the Théâtre du Soleil (Vincennes).

of his daughter rather than with Clytemnestra's killing of her husband, Mnouchkine's production raises a question which otherwise tends not to be voiced or even formulated: Why are Orestes and, even more pointedly, Electra—another daughter of Clytemnestra and Agamemnon—so bent on avenging the murder of the father who has sacrificed their sister? In this light, the final play of Aeschylus's trilogy takes on new meaning. The long drawn-out struggle between Athena and the Furies becomes riveting in its implication that the working through of conflicts among women holds a key to replacing violence with speaking, bringing private feuds into public places, and healing wounds which otherwise fester from generation to generation—-in short, to establishing democracy and civilization.

Let me be more specific. The Furies, played as a group of old women who unleash a seemingly boundless and high-spirited energy, will not let go of their anger at what has happened to Clytemnestra and, by implication, Iphigenia as well. Athena, the goddess born from the head of Zeus, the young woman whose mother was swallowed by her father, is, as she says, "wholly of the father" (the patriarchy) and unequivocally committed to realizing his (its) projects. As Athena arrives again and again to work through her struggle with the old women, to tame their wild energy and bring them into the city as the Eumenides (the good spirits), the visual impact of her repeated returning conveys the difficulty and the urgency of this reconciliation.

In *Civilization and Its Discontents*, Freud asks the question: Why have men created a culture in which they live with such discomfort? Here I raise corollary questions about the relationship between inner and outer worlds: How do maintain a coherent inner world within an outer world that is patriarchal? How can women breathe psychologically within this civilization?

REPEATING, REMEMBERING, AND WORKING THROUGH

At the end of ten years' research into women's psychological development, I remembered the hysterical women of the late nineteenth

century, the women Freud called his "teachers" (Appignanesi and Forrester, 1992). I reread Breuer's description of Anna O.:

> She was markedly intelligent, with an astonishingly quick grasp of things
> and penetrating intuition. She possessed a powerful intellect. . . . She
> had great poetic and imaginative gifts, which were under the control
> of a sharp and critical common sense. Owing to this latter quality she
> was *completely unsuggestible*; she was only influenced by arguments,
> never by mere assertions. Her willpower was energetic, tenacious and
> persistent; sometimes it reached the pitch of an obstinacy which only
> gave way out of kindness and regard for other people. One of her es-
> sential traits was sympathetic kindness. . . . The element of sexuality
> was astonishingly undeveloped in her. (emphasis in original; Breuer
> and Freud, 1893–1895/1974, p. 73)

When Anna fell ill at the age of twenty-one, she was not able to speak,
losing words, losing language, not able to see or to hear, not able to move,
suffering from severe hallucinations and suicidal impulses, and alternat-
ing between two states of consciousness which were entirely separate
from one another: a melancholy and anxious state in which she was present and seemed normal, and a state of "absence" in which she "lost" time
and could not remember. In her states of absence, Anna was "not herself," but wild, naughty, abusive, throwing cushions at people, pulling
buttons off her bedclothes and linens, hallucinating, seemingly crazy.
Breuer notes,

> she would complain of having "lost" some time and would remark
> upon the gap in her train of conscious thoughts. . . . At moments when
> her mind was quite clear she would complain of the profound darkness
> in her head, of not being able to think, of becoming blind and deaf, of
> having two selves, a real one and an evil one which forced her to be-
> have badly, and so on.
>
> In the afternoons, she would fall into a somnolent state which lasted
> till about an hour after sunset. She would then wake up and complain
> that something was tormenting her—or rather, she would keep re-
> peating in the impersonal form "tormenting, tormenting." For along-
> side of the development of the contractures there appeared a deep-go-

ing functional disorganization of her speech. . . . In the process of time she became almost completely deprived of words. (pp. 76–77)

Breuer, observing that Anna had felt very much offended by something but had determined not to speak about it, encouraged her to speak and offered a resonant presence. And when, in this resonant space, Anna discovered that she could enter her absences and speak and see and hear for herself, she had discovered what she called "a talking cure." Given that voice depends on resonance, that speaking depends on listening and being heard, loss of voice was a symptom of loss of relationship. It was a relationship that enabled Anna to regain her voice, and it was the recovery of her voice that set her free.

Freud observed that loss of voice was the most common symptom of hysteria, and, given this observation, hysteria itself becomes a sign of a relational impasse or crisis. The resonances set off by the voices of the hysterical women clearly stirred the men who were treating them. Describing the character of his patient Fraulein Elisabeth von R., Freud notes "the features which one meets with so frequently in hysterical people," citing as typical "her giftedness, her ambition, her moral sensibility, her excessive demand for love which, to begin with, found satisfaction in her family, and the independence of her nature which went beyond the feminine ideal and found expression in a considerable amount of obstinacy, pugnacity and reserve" (Breuer and Freud, 1893–95, p. 231).

When these intelligent, sensitive, stubborn, and mute young women began speaking of incestuous relationships with their fathers, Freud wrote to Fliess that he had arrived at *Caput Nili*—the head of the Nile; he had traced the origins of hysteria to childhood sexual trauma and linked neurosis with the structure of relationships between men and women and children in patriarchy. The difficulty which the women experienced in keeping inner and outer worlds connected, however, now began to affect their physicians. It was not possible to take in the inner worlds of hysterical women, or, in contemporary terms, borderline personalities, and continue to live and function in the same way in the outer world of civilization. Psychoanalysis, as it developed in relationship with women who were teaching Freud to see the close connection between body and psyche and the borders between inner and outer worlds, was a radical inquiry. The talking cure was deceptively simple, given its ability to heal dissociation.

In 1896, the year following the publication of *Studies on Hysteria*, Freud's father dies, and on the night after the funeral, he dreams that he is in a barbershop where a sign on the wall says: "You are requested to close the eyes." Freud writes to Fliess about this dream, saying, "the old man's death has affected me deeply." Shortly thereafter he begins his self-analysis.

The following year, in the letter to Fliess in which Freud explains that he no longer believes in his neurotica (theory of the neuroses), he expresses his "surprise that in all cases, the *father*, not excluding my own, had to be accused of being perverse," adding, "the realization of the unexpected frequency of hysteria, with precisely the same conditions prevailing in each, whereas surely such widespread perversions against children are not very probable" (p. 264, emphasis in original). His "certain insight" was "that there are no indications of reality in the unconscious, so that one cannot distinguish between truth and fiction that has been cathected with affect." The sexual trauma, which had seemed a reality, might more probably be regarded as a sexual fantasy (p. 264).

Psychoanalysis would predict that once Freud says he will not talk about incest, he will talk about nothing else. And, in fact, in his major theoretical work—*The Interpretation of Dreams* (1900)—he places the Oedipus story, an incest story, as the cornerstone of psychoanalysis. In doing so, however, Freud introduces a radical displacement in narrative voice and perspective. In place of the young woman speaking of an incestuous relationship with her father, Freud inserts the boy fantasizing an incestuous relationship with his mother. The shift in emphasis from reality to fantasy, from outer world to inner world, follows this shift in narration. Replacing the more frequently occurring father-daughter incest with the less common and more taboo incest between mother and son, Freud turns the focus of attention from the voices of hysterical women to the situation of the boy—the young Oedipus—who in time may grow up to be Oedipus Rex, the incestuous father.

The Dora case—"A Fragment of an Analysis of a Case of Hysteria"—becomes so tumultuous in part because it marks the return of the voice Freud has repressed. Dora comes for analysis in the year that Freud published *The Interpretation of Dreams*, at a time when he was seeking confirmation for his theory of dreams. And Dora, beside herself at the thought that her father did not believe her or take her seriously, speaks to Freud through two dreams.

In the first dream, the house is on fire and Dora's father is standing by her bed and wakes her up. She wants to save her mother's jewel case, but her father insists that they leave the house at once, saying that he cares only for the safety of his children. They hurry downstairs and as soon as she is outside of the house, Dora wakes up. Freud maintains a deaf ear to what seems a thinly encoded incest narrative, or rather insists that this incestuous drama represents Dora's wish, Dora's fantasy.

In response, Dora dreams that her father is dead. She receives a letter from her mother telling her of the death, and begins an arduous journey home, arriving after everyone has left for the cemetery. Then, climbing the stairs, she "went calmly to her room, and began reading a big book that lay on her writing table" (Freud, 1977/1905, p. 140). Initially Dora forgets this final dream segment—-and while Freud focuses on the encyclopedia as signifying Dora's secret pursuit of sexual knowledge, the detail of the writing table suggests that Dora may now have come to the realization that the encyclopedia does not contain her story and that if she wants her story, her sexual experience, to become knowledge, she may have to write it herself. Shortly after this dream, Dora leaves the analysis.

In the *Three Essays on the Theory of Sexuality*, published in 1905—-the same year Freud releases the Dora case for publication—-Freud writes, "the erotic life of men alone has become accessible to research. That of women—partly owing to the stunting effects of civilized conditions and partly owing to their secretiveness and insincerity—is still veiled in an impenetrable obscurity" (p. 151). Freud has left his hysterical women patients, the women whose voices he had encouraged, up to a point. The stubborn, independent, unsuggestible hysterics who resisted Freud and were his teachers will give way to "Freud's women," as psychoanalysis internalizes the structures of patriarchy. Following the turn of the century, as the focus of psychoanalytic attention increasingly shifts away from adolescence and to early childhood, the seeing and speaking young women became screened or hidden by images of the Madonna mothers and silent infants—the iconography in Western culture of female devotion and compliance.

Discussing the case of Elisabeth von R., Freud (1895) observed that "her love had become separated from her knowledge." This dissociation had entered psychoanalysis. The love of their women patients that is evident in Breuer and Freud's early case histories was connected with momentous discovery, including the psychological causes of physical symptoms, the method of free association, and the power of the talking cure to heal dissociation. But this knowledge depended on relationship. Writing about his treatment of Elisabeth von R., Freud reveals the wellsprings of empathy—his willingness to enter into her feelings: "If we put greater misfortune to one side and enter into a girl's feelings, we cannot refrain from deep human sympathy with Fraulein Elisabeth" (p. 212). It may be that the sexual implications or overtones of such entry overwhelmed the knowledge gained through such connection with women, or perhaps this knowledge was so profoundly upsetting that it readily led to the reimposition of domination, at times through sexual conquest. In Dora's case, Freud struggles between entering into a girl's feelings and drawing a girl and her feelings into the framework of history—the framework of the Oedipus story. Dora's brief analysis plays out the struggle of a young woman's initiation into a patriarchal culture, and Freud, in publishing his fragmentary case history, records the ambivalence and in the end the compulsion of the father in her sacrifice.

But, predictably, the repressed returns. The late nineteenth-century drama between women and psychoanalysis, with its central struggle over the question of truth and reality, has been reenacted at the end of the twentieth century. Again, women were encouraged to speak and, in resonant relationship, the power of the talking cure became apparent. Again, women's voices exposed a problem of relationship—an incidence of incest between fathers and daughters that seemed so widespread as to appear improbable. And again a radical skepticism set in. The discovery of a profound and troubling connection between inner and outer worlds has again been followed by the claim that Freud makes in the case of Dora: the claim that he knows her inner world better than she does.

A TALKING CURE

The issue is explicit: the cure for not speaking is relationship. Because voice depends on resonance, speaking depends on relationship. The breach between inner and outer worlds or the dissociation from parts of the inner world can be healed through a talking cure.

Normi Noel, a voice teacher who trained with Kristin Linklater, joined the Strengthening Healthy Resistance and Courage in Girls project to observe what happens to girls' voices at the edge of adolescence (see Gilligan, Rogers, and Noel, 1992). Drawing on Linklater's *Freeing the Natural Voice* (1976), Noel makes the following observations: "Linklater defines vibrations as needing surfaces to re-sound or amplify the initial impulse to speak. The body creates its own resonators. We build theaters to amplify the truth of the human voice. Musical instruments require surfaces and enclosed spaces to create more vibration. . . . Linklater's mantra for all young actors studying voice is that 'tension murders vibration,' while 'vibrations thrive on attention'; with attention, the voice grows in power and range to reveal the truth" (Noel, 1995).

In the course of the three-year project with girls, Noel picked up and followed the psychological dynamics that lead the impulse of the voice to go off sound. She named a series of steps leading from full speaking voice, to half-voice, to breathiness and into silence. In the silence, Noel picked up the almost imperceptible vibration of the impulse to speak, which remained alive, vibrating in what she called an inner "cello world or resonating chamber" (Noel, 1995). Keeping a journal to record her observations, Noel writes about resonance:

Just as the acoustics for the strengthening of sound require certain physical properties, so too do the voices of the girls depend on a sympathetic "sounding board" or environment. Gilligan warns of the risk to girls around eleven or twelve who enter a patriarchal culture. It is filled with a dissonance that separates intellect from feeling. When there is no longer a "place" or "room" to strengthen their truth or practice speaking directly what they know, the girls then leave the vibrations of their speaking voice and move from breathiness to silence. In this silence, an inner cello world or resonating chamber keeps alive the energy of initial thought/feelings, preserving an integrity that risks everything if taken back onto the speaking voice in a culture still unable to provide a resonance for such clarity, subtlety and power. (Noel, 1995)

Noel concludes that by keeping alive the initial impulse to speak in an inner "cello world" or "resonating chamber," girls at adolescence create an inner sanctuary for a voice that holds a truth that others do not want to hear—a speaking voice that finds no resonance in the outer world. In this way, girls becoming women find a way "to hold their truth by *not* speaking," and their speaking voice becomes a cover for and at the same time gives off soundings of a "hidden world [that] women have rooted themselves in and survived" the dampening effects of a patriarchal language and culture (Noel, 1995).

Iris is seventeen.[3] A senior at the Laurel School in Cleveland, she has come to Harvard with two classmates to interview Lyn Mikel Brown and myself about our research on women's psychology and girls' development. We have been interviewing girls and going on retreats with women at the school for the past five years, and now that our project is ending, they want to know about the book we are writing, and also about our methods and our findings (see Brown and Gilligan, 1992). As we settle into a formal interview rhythm—the girls ask us questions and we respond—I notice that there is no evidence of a very different conversation about the research that took place in the course of a day-long retreat with

3. To protect confidentiality, I have changed girls' names and identifying details.

their entire class the previous June. Listening to their questions, I find that I have a dizzying sensation—it is as if the intense and impassioned conversation which took place that day had never happened.

Iris's questions were about standards—what standards did we use to measure women's psychological health and girls' development? I look at her questioningly, curious as to why she is interested in standards, and she explains that she finds standards comforting, that she likes to know where she stands. And by the commonly used measures of psychological health and development, Iris is doing very well. She has been accepted by the competitive college that is her first choice and chosen by her classmates as their representative. She describes her family as loving and as supporting her in her aspirations. Lively, articulate, engaging, and responsive, Iris seems to be flourishing.

At the end of the session, after the girls have turned off their tape recorder, we continue to sit around the table and talk as the light lengthens at the end of the afternoon. The conversation returns to the young girls in the study, and we tell the stories illustrating their outspokenness, their courage in relationships, their willingness to speak their minds and their hearts. Iris suddenly leans forward and says: "If I were to say what I was feeling and thinking, no one would want to be with me—my voice would be too loud." And then, flustered by what she is saying, she adds, by way of explanation: "But you have to have relationships."

I ask Iris: "If you are not saying what you are feeling and thinking, then where are you in these relationships?" Immediately it is clear that she also sees the paradox in what she is saying: she has given up relationship for the sake of having "relationships," muting her voice so that "she" can be with other people. The words *self* and *relationship* lose their meaning and the feeling of impasse becomes palpable as Iris, her face momentarily shadowed, looks into a relational impasse, a psychological blind alley.

The paradoxical sacrifice of relationship for the sake of relationships is the core dynamic of initiation into a patriarchal social order. Resetting the relationship between inner and outer worlds, it marks a definitive turn in psychological development—the internalization of the existing social order. Jean Baker Miller has formulated this paradoxical sacrifice of relationship in a struggle to make and maintain relationships as the core dynamic of what has been called psychopathology—-a confusing term because while the suffering is psychological, the pathology is relationship, stemming from a disconnection between inner and outer worlds that seemingly has to be maintained. Linking women's psychology with empirical studies of girls' development, my colleagues and I have heard girls describe this relational paradox, and we have witnessed the onset of dissociative processes as a response to their experience of impasse. Moved by the girls' resistance, their resilience and courage in fighting to maintain their voices and stay in relationship, we interpreted dissociative processes as a brilliant but costly solution to what seemed an insoluble problem: how to maintain both voice and relationships. Dissociation was a way of maintaining a coherent inner world within an outer world that for many women was fundamentally incoherent: at odds with what they knew to be true on the basis of their own experience (see Gilligan, Brown, and Rogers, 1990; Gilligan, 1990a, 1990b; Brown and Gilligan, 1992; Rogers, 1993; also Gilligan, Rogers, and Noel, 1992; Gilligan and Rogers, 1993; Rogers, Brown, and Tappan, 1994; Taylor, Gilligan, and Sullivan, 1996).

Anne Frank, in what turns out to be her final diary entry, says that she has gained the reputation of being a "little bundle of contradictions." She writes that the description fits her, but then asks, "What does contradiction mean?" observing that, "Like so many words, it can mean two things, contradiction from without and contradiction from within" (p. 697). Giving words to her experience, Anne distinguishes between two forms of relational impasse: one coming from an experience of confrontation and leading her to become known as unpleasant, and one coming from an experience of inner division and leading to shame, confusion, and conflict.

Contradiction from without, although difficult, is familiar; it is "the ordinary not giving in easily, always knowing best, getting in the last word, enfin, all the unpleasant qualities for which I am renowned" (p. 697).

Contradiction from within, however, is shameful and hidden: "Nobody knows about it; that's my own secret . . . I have, as it were, a dual personality" (p. 697). Anne describes the two Annes. One is exuberant, cheerful, sensual and insouciant: she does not mind "a kiss, an embrace, a dirty joke" (p. 697). This is the Anne "people find insufferable," the Anne she calls "bad." The other Anne is "better, deeper, purer"; she is the "nice Anne," the "quiet Anne," the "serious Anne," and also the Anne who is silent and frozen. She never appears or speaks in public, because "They'll laugh at me, think I'm ridiculous, sentimental, not take me in earnest. I'm used to not being taken seriously but it's only the light-hearted Anne that's used to it and can bear it; the deeper Anne is too frail for it" (p. 698). In contrast to the vital but seemingly superficial and bad Anne, Anne characterizes the deeper, silent, and frozen Anne as good.

Like Nina's rejection of her vibrant Civil War story in favor of the more conventional and pallid romantic adventure or the clever story about the pen, like Edith Wharton's dismissal of her early short stories as "quite dreadful," like Iphigenia's abandonment of her appeal for relationship in the realization that it has become hopeless and shameful, Anne Frank is struggling against a vital part of herself, and the question of standards or judgment, like the question of relationship, becomes intensely confusing.

Melanie Klein and the object relations theorists would trace the origins of this splitting into a good and bad self to the preoedipal period of infancy and early childhood—a time seemingly outside civilization. And they would consider the splitting or what Erikson has called the "totalism" of adolescence—the adolescent's penchant for either/or, all-or-nothing formulations—as a recapitulation of an earlier developmental process, a revisiting of early conflicts around sexuality and relationships and an opportunity to work them through differently. In the case of young women, however, beginning with the hysterics, adolescence seems to witness the onset of a problem of relationship or to bring a problem of relationship to crisis—a crisis that cannot be worked through on an intrapsychic level. The splitting or dissociation, rather than being a naturally occurring developmental phenomenon, appears instead to be a costly although necessary psychological adaptation to a deeply confusing split in reality—-the division between inner and outer worlds, and also within the inner world that is essential to the reproduction of patriarchy.

From somewhere outside the division within herself that Anne Frank describes, a voice speaks in direct first-person about voice, honesty, and the seeming impossibility of becoming herself with other people.

> I never utter my real feelings about anything. If I'm to be quite honest, I must admit that it does hurt me—-that I try terribly hard to change myself but that I'm always fighting against a more powerful enemy. A voice sobs within me: "There you are, that's what's become of you, you're uncharitable, you look supercilious and peevish, people you meet dislike you and all because you won't listen to the advice given you by your own better half." Oh, I would like to listen, but it doesn't work, if I'm quiet and serious they all think that it's a new comedy and then I have to get out of it by turning it into a joke, not to mention my own family, who are sure to think I'm ill, make me swallow pills for headaches and sedatives and criticize me for being in a bad mood. I can't keep that up, if I'm watched to that extent I start by getting snappy, then unhappy, and finally I twist my heart round so that the bad is on the outside and the good is on the inside and keep on trying to find a way of becoming what I would so like to be and what I could be, if—there weren't any other people living in the world. (p. 699)

As Anne records her efforts to bring her inner world into the outer world, she describes herself as embattled from without and from within.

When I taught with Erik Erikson at Harvard in the late 1960s, he was working on *Gandhi's Truth* and actively exploring the relationship between satyagraha—the force of truth that is at the heart of nonviolent resistance—and the power of truth that leads to psychological healing. Erikson's belief that one cannot understand a life outside of history, that life-history and history are two sides of a coin, led him to search for the creative intersection, the place where life-history and history join. In Erikson's analysis, the young Martin Luther, unable to act effectively against the corruption of authority in his childhood family, took on the corruption of authority that was the central public problem of his time and initiated the Reformation.

For more than a century now, girls have been suffering from a corruption of relationship that they often cannot address within the family. Like the corruption of authority in Luther's time, this corruption is widespread, part of a cultural fabric that is rotten. Joining life and history, women have initiated a transformation of relationships that is comparable in scope to the Reformation. But this is the point where relationship comes into tension with relationships—the point at which women's voices begin to sound too loud.

A THEORETICAL FRAME

Freud conceptualized the tension between civilization and psychological health and development as forcing a "compromise formation"—some accommodation between inner and outer worlds. This compromise formation marked the resolution of the Oedipus complex, the relational crisis of boys' early childhood, and it left a psychological scar that was a seedbed for neurosis. The wound, although it is generally not conceptualized in these terms, came from giving up relationship; it marked the tearing away from or walling off of the most vulnerable parts of the inner world, in a self-defeating and often inchoate attempt to protect the capacity to love.

A substantial body of evidence, gathered over the course of a century, indicates that girls are psychologically stronger and more resilient than boys throughout the childhood years (see Gilligan, 1991, 1996). Clinical, developmental, and epidemiological data also show that girls' resilience is at risk in adolescence. In adolescence there is a sudden high incidence of depression among girls; an outbreak of eating disorders, suicide attempts, and learning problems—all of which suggest difficulty in making or maintaining the connection between inner and outer worlds.

Girls' resilience at the time of adolescence—their fight to maintain their voice and stay in relationship—provides the grounds for new theory because it renders articulate what otherwise remains inchoate: the psychological break between inner and outer worlds that signifies the internalization of patriarchy. Listening to girls' voices at the time of this dissociation, hearing knowing yield to not knowing, it became possible to see a psychological blind spot in the making and to hear the beginnings of what George Eliot called "the roar on the other side of silence (see Belenky et al., 1986; Gilligan, 1990a, 1990b; Noel, 1995; Rogers, 1995). Then it becomes evident to what extent most theories of human psychology and human development have incorporated into their very formulation the civilization of the Oresteia and the Oedipus tragedy.

Within this cultural framework, a separation of inner from outer world occurs typically for boys in early childhood (between, roughly, the ages of three and five) and constitutes a cultural initiation. It is tied in with male identity and seems essential to the young boy's claim to his manhood—his "symbolic castration" which signifies his willingness to sacrifice his physical and psychological integrity in order to claim his membership in a patriarchal civilization. In short, the separation of inner from outer world in young boys is a culturally mandated separation which becomes psychologically necessary if boys are to be able to make and maintain relationships in the world, at the same time that it creates the most powerful obstacle to their capacity for relationship and intimacy. Symbolically, this separation of boys from an inner world associated with mothers is represented by the freeing of Orestes from the Furies. Psychologically, this separation or walling off of the innermost parts of the inner world makes it possible for a boy to be hurt without feeling hurt, to leave without feeling sadness or loss.

Boys' early childhood separation constitutes a process of initiation that is essential to the structuring and maintenance of a patriarchal social order, and it ensures the continuation of that order, generation after generation. A boy's resistance to this separation in patriarchal cultures leads men, women, and the boy himself to question and doubt his masculinity, making him an object of shame. Men live with discomfort in the civilization they have created because of this disconnection from the inner world. The dissociation of self from relationship leaves, as Freud describes in *Civilization and Its Discontents* and as both self and relational psychologists have substantially elaborated, an unsatisfied and unsatisfiable yearning for connection, an inner emptiness, a longing for relationship which developmental psychologists have now discovered is grounded in the infant's experience of relationship, but which, following infancy, seems illusory or culturally proscribed as shameful.

Girls' extraordinary love and knowledge of the human world throughout childhood can be understood as reflecting a continuing connection between inner and outer worlds. Otherwise, it is hard to explain how girls know what they know or can sustain their openness and vulnerability. Girls' full initiation into a patriarchal "not knowing" and "invulnerability" tends not to occur until puberty and adolescence, when girls are under intense pressure from without and within to separate the inner world and take in an outer world that changes what they will feel and think and know. The contrast between Iphigenia's two speeches, or Nina's early and later stories, or the two conversations with Iris and her classmates captures this turn—this fixing of one's heart and mind.

The fact that boys, beginning in early childhood, are more at risk than girls for depression, suicide attempts, accidents and injuries, bed-wetting, learning disorders, and various other forms of "out of touch" and "out of control" behavior, all of which suggest a rift between inner and outer worlds, together with the fact that for girls this rift and the attendant signs of psychological distress occur more frequently at adolescence, poses a developmental and clinical puzzle that clarifies a profound intersection of psychology and culture (see Gilligan, 1996).

In adolescence, girls often fight for relationship, and, following a pattern that begins in antiquity, when this appeal finds no resonance and becomes shamefully ineffective, young women in a variety of ways sacrifice or sequester themselves. Discovering the difficulty or seeming impossibility of keeping a vital inner world, young women are likely to bury that part of themselves which they most want and love.

Beginning then with the voice of Iphigenia, as Euripides heard or imagined her, a search for resonance—for relationship—is vital to women coming of age in a patriarchal culture. The same is true for men as well. In the absence of resonance or the possibility of relationship, the hope for relationship dims, and young women, like boys, often becoming hysterical in the process. Or, they seemingly solve the problem of relationship by tuning their voices in the dominant key. A talking cure— a listening cure—is then a deceptively simple and profoundly radical psychological intervention. Relying on the power of association to free the voice by providing resonance, it beings into the outer world an inner world that has been muted or that has come to sound off-key. The talking cure, relying on voice and resonance, moves through the walls set up by dissociation. In this way, the talking cure has the power to undo the initiation into patriarchy.

Generation after generation of girls becoming young women have paused at the moment of their initiation. Shocked to see an impending loss of relationship, drawn by the allure of relationships, they may hesitate and take their bearings, leaving a psychological map of an intensely volatile political situation. When sexuality—the guide to pleasure that lies in the materiality of the body—and love become confused with violation, girls face a difficult and dangerous passage. But when girls becoming young women and women becoming mothers counterpose their experience of relationship to the patriarchal construction of relationships, they precipitate in the dailiness of their living, whether at home or in the city, a crisis with far-reaching psychological and political implications. Then, if we can remember rather than repeat the past, if we can join rather than repress the resistance, the working through of this crisis holds the potential for love and may create the foundation for a new civilization.

REFERENCES

Aeschylus. 1956. *The Oresteia*. Volume I in *The Complete Greek Tragedies*. Ed. D. Greene and R. Lattimore. Chicago: University of Chicago Press.
Appignanesi, L., and Forrester, J. 1992. *Freud's Women*. New York: Basic Books.
Belenky, M., Clinchy, B., Goldberger, N., and Tarule, J. 1986. *Women's Ways*

of Knowing: The Development of Self, Voice, and Mind. New York: Basic Books.

Breuer, J., and Freud, S. 1893–95/1974. *Studies on Hysteria.* Trans. James and Alix Strachey. London: Penguin Books.

Brown, L. M., and Gilligan, C. 1992. *Meeting at the Crossroads: Women's Psychology and Girls' Development.* New York: Ballantine Books.

Erikson, E. 1958. *Young Man Luther.* New York: W. W. Norton.

———. 1969. *Gandhi's Truth.* New York: W. W. Norton.

Euripides. 1958. *Iphigenia in Aulis.* Volume IV in *The Complete Greek Tragedies.* Ed. D. Greene and R. Lattimore. Chicago: University of Chicago Press.

Frank, Anne. 1989/1942–44. *Diary. The Critical Edition.* New York: Doubleday.

Freud, Sigmund. 1887–1904/1985. *The Complete Letters of Sigmund Freud to Wilhelm Fliess.* Trans. and ed. Jeffrey Moussaieff Masson. Cambridge, Mass.: Harvard University Press.

———. 1905/1977. *Case Histories I: "Dora" and "Little Hans."* Trans. Alix and James Strachey. London: Penguin Books.

———. 1900. *The Interpretation of Dreams. Standard Edition,* 4–5.

———. 1905. *Three Essays on the Theory of Sexuality. Standard Edition,* 7:125–244.

———. 1929–30. *Civilization and Its Discontents. Standard Edition.* 21:59–145.

Gilligan, Carol. 1990a. "Teaching Shakespeare's Sister: Notes from the Underground of Female Adolescence." In *Making Connections.* Ed. C. Gilligan, N. Lyons, and T. Hanmer. Cambridge, Mass.: Harvard University Press.

———. 1990b. "Joining the Resistance: Psychology, Politics, Girls and Women." *Michigan Quarterly Review,* 29:4.

———. 1991. "Women's Psychological Development: Implications for Psychotherapy." In *Women, Girls and Psychotherapy: Reframing Resistance.* Ed. C. Gilligan, A. Rogers, and D. Tolman. Birmingham, N.Y.: Haworth Press.

———. 1996. "The Centrality of Relationship in Human Development: A Puzzle, Some Evidence, and a Theory." In *Development and Vulnerability in Close Relationships.* Ed. G. Noam and K. Fischer. Hillside, N.J.: Erlbaum.

Gilligan, Carol, Brown, Lyn Mikel, and Rogers, Annie. 1990. "Psyche Embedded: A Place for Body, Relationships and Culture in Personality

Theory." In *Studying Persons and Lives.* Ed. A. Rabin et al. New York: Springer.

Gilligan, Carol, and Rogers, Annie. 1993. "Strengthening Healthy Resistance and Courage in Girls: A Developmental Study and a Prevention Project." Final Project Report to the Lilly Endowment. Cambridge, Mass.: Harvard Project on Women's Psychology and Girls' Development.

Gilligan, Carol, Rogers, Annie, and Noel, Normi. 1992. "Cartography of a Lost Time: Women, Girls and Relationships." Paper presented at the Cambridge Hospital and Stone Center conference "Learning from Women," Boston, April 1992. In *Working Papers,* 1993. Cambridge, Mass.: Harvard Project on Women's Psychology and Girls' Development.

Gilligan, James. 1996. *Violence: Our Deadly Epidemic and Its Causes.* New York: Putnam.

Klein, Melanie. 1975. *The Writings of Melanie Klein.* London: Hogarth Press and the Institute of Psychoanalysis.

Kohut, Heinz. 1971. *The Analysis of the Self.* New York: International Universities Press.

Linklater, Kristin. 1976. *Freeing the Natural Voice.* New York: Drama Books.

Miller, Jean Baker. 1988. "Connections, Disconnections and Violations." *Work in Progress,* 33. Wellesley, Mass.: Stone Center Working Paper Series.

Noel, Normi. 1995. Unpublished journal.

Renik, Owen. In press. "The Ideal of the Anonymous Analyst and the Problem of Self-Disclosure." *Psychoanalytic Quarterly.*

Rogers, Annie. 1993. "Voice, Play, and a Practice of Ordinary Courage in Girls' and Women's Lives." *Harvard Educational Review,* 63 (3): 265–295.

———. 1995. "Exiled Voices: Dissociation and Repression in Women's Narratives of Trauma." *Work in Progress,* 67. Wellesley, Mass.: Stone Center Working Paper Series.

Taylor, Jill McLean, Gilligan, Carol, and Sullivan, Amy. In press. *Between Voice and Silence: Women and Girls, Race and Relationship.* Cambridge, Mass.: Harvard University Press.

Wolff, Cynthia Griffin. 1977. *A Feast of Words.* New York: Oxford University Press.

Woolf, Virginia. 1921/1981. "An Unwritten Novel." In *A Haunted House and Other Stories.* London: Grafton Press.

Anton Obholzer, M.D.

■ 9 Psychoanalytic Institutions in a
Changing World

I should like to share with you a short description of a state of mind
that is very common nowadays as an approach to society and its institutions. The unknown writer captures the essence of the process that we
all face in our attempts to maintain standards and stand by ideals of conduct and practice—ideals that have taken decades to define.

An Operational Research Report on ———'s *Fifth Symphony*
For considerable periods the four oboe players had nothing to do.
The numbers should be reduced, and the work spread more evenly
over the whole of the concert, thus eliminating peaks of activity.

All the twelve first violins were playing identical notes. This seems
unnecessary duplication. The staff of this section should be drastically
cut; if a large volume of sound is required, it could be obtained by
means of electronic amplifier apparatus.

Much effort was absorbed in the playing of demisemiquavers. This seems an excessive refinement. It is recommended that all notes should be rounded up to the nearest semiquaver. If this were done, it would be possible to use trainees and lower grade operatives more extensively.

There seems to be too much repetition of some musical passages. Scores should be drastically pruned. No useful purpose is served by repeating on the horns a passage which has already been handled by the strings. It is estimated that if all redundant passages were eliminated, the whole concert time of two hours could be reduced to twenty minutes, and there would be no need for an interval.

The conductor agrees generally with these recommendations, but expresses the opinion that there might be some falling-off in box-office receipts. In that unlikely event, it should be possible to close sections of the auditorium entirely, with a consequent saving of overhead expense—lighting, attendants, etc.

Many of us identify with the conductor struggling to find a way of keeping our orchestra and its music going when besieged by accountants, health insurance officials, and public officials concerned with "reforming" health services. Dealing with apparatchiks is bad enough. But unfortunately these officials represent more than just themselves and their institutions. They represent a changing world system. Thus, just as in our field of work the symptom has to be seen against the overall whole, so too these changes must be read against the background of a changing world.

SOME THOUGHTS ON CHANGES IN THE GLOBAL SYSTEM

As psychoanalysts we generally shy away from attempting to apply psychoanalytic thinking to the world situation. The path of this type of exploration is littered with the wrecks of psychobiographies and other works that have done little for our understanding of history and much for the low esteem in which our profession is held in some quarters. Freud himself was not averse to writing in this area. Note his formidable *Civilization and Its Discontents* (1930), *Moses and Monotheism* (1939), and *Totem and Taboo* (1913), though the last met with criticism from anthropologists.

Some subsequent writers have fared better in their reception and in their capacities to illuminate societal and institutional processes. I am thinking of Roger Money-Kyrle's *Man's Picture of His World* (1961); of Henry Dicks's work on the Nazi war criminals (1972), and later on his work with marriages and couples (1967); of Wilfred Bion's *Experiences in Groups* (1961). There is also the tradition of sociologists such as Ken Rice (1970), Eric Miller (1993), and Gordon Lawrence (1979), all of whom at one stage were at the Tavistock Institute of Human Relations. And, nearer home and more recently, we have Edward Shapiro and Wesley Carr's *Lost in Familiar Places* (1991).

Given these precedents, I think it worthwhile to make an attempt at viewing the present-day world situation from a psychoanalytic perspective, and linking it to the processes we are experiencing in our profession.

The main change that has happened is that certainty has left the world scene. There was a time when societies knew, often with almost delusional clarity, what was good and what was bad, whether it referred to nations or to political or to social systems. We might each use different terminology to describe this phenomenon of clarity, better described as "delusional pseudo-clarity," but we would all agree that we are talking about very primitive mental mechanisms. In essence, we are talking of splitting mechanisms, resulting in good qualities being attributed to "us" and bad qualities to "them." Melanie Klein's ideas (1946), in particular, were very influential in this area. Building on Freud's earlier work, she elaborated the concepts of splitting and projective identification as early mental mechanisms essential for the development of the child and remaining with the individual throughout life. As described by Klein, the child develops defensive mechanisms of splitting and projective identification in order to avoid experiencing intolerable confusion and ambiguity. These mechanisms lessen the confusion, replacing it with pseudo-clarity about good and bad, us and them. This creates an illusory sense of movement and relief. In line with this dynamic, there was a time when it was quite clear on the international scene who the "thems" were. But this system of global certainty has now broken down, and we are hard-pressed to agree on who the "thems" of the present day are.

There have been attempts to find replacement bad objects for the East-West split, but the minor figures that have been thrown up and dwelt upon by the world's press have not been substantial enough to resurrect the clear-cut global political military split of the recent past. The political ideologies that have accompanied some of the previous power blocks—Marxism or various forms of Communism and socialism—have receded as a threat and no longer lend themselves so comfortably as convenient receptacles for processes of projective identification.

The external factors that have made for and encouraged global splitting mechanisms as a way of dealing with our own internal confusions—be they national, group, or individual—are no longer as available. As a consequence, we have had to fall back on resolving matters within ourselves. I am postulating a change in the world order in which the dynamic focus has shifted from global to domestic concerns. I am using the terms *global* and *domestic* to describe not only a change in magnitude and venue, but also an altered state of mind. We have shifted from attention to ideals and global perspectives to more circumscribed, local thinking. This is captured in the "report" at the beginning of this chapter, and could be paraphrased as knowing the cost of everything and the value of nothing. We now focus our attention on what is going on in our national systems—health, education, law and order, and business.

I believe this shift to be one of the factors responsible for the winds of change that we are all caught up in. The same splitting and related mechanisms previously active on the global front are now at play in smaller domestic forums, and have become manifestations of our everyday life and work. "Good" and "bad" and other such oversimplifications and indices of pseudo-clarity are constantly present and at risk of settling onto our professional, educational, and other substructures of society. They lead to much ill-informed debate that has nothing to do with the issues at hand and everything to do with displaced societal issues in a new forum.

Not only are all professional groupings under attack, but there has also been a resurgence of racial and religious intolerance in many parts of the globe. We have shifted from a primitive macro system to a reenactment of the same mechanisms in many micro systems.

There are other factors that add to the complexity and richness of the picture. Wilfred Bion wrote his classic book, *Experiences in Groups* (1961), outlining his view about the states of mind that groups fall into. He differentiated the group as an entity from the individuals in the group, whom he saw only as aspects of the whole. Pierre Turquet (1975) later elaborated this by describing the individual being taken over by the group.

For the purposes of this chapter, Bion's notion of group refers not only to a collection of individuals, but also to institutions and larger collectives. Thus communities and the nation would be subject to the same processes. Bion suggested that group functioning occurred along a spectrum, with what he called "basic assumption" group functioning at one end and "work group" functioning at the other. Where the group functioning rested at any one time depended on a variety of factors, including the mechanisms by which underlying anxiety was dealt with, the clarity of task, and the use of management structures. The essence of the basic assumption group mode was that it was subject to primitive psychic mechanisms similar to splitting and projective identification.

Bion detailed three forms of basic assumption functioning: dependency, fight-flight, and pairing. These were unconscious modes of group behavior in which the group behaves as if it were operating on the assumption, for example, that gratifying dependency needs would substitute for work.

The collapse of the world system of projective identification through the fall of global power blocks illuminates the dynamics of basic assumption dependency. One of the key power blocks was the Marxist-Communist-socialist block. This was, in essence, a dependency culture, or, in Bion's terms, a manifestation of basic assumption dependency, where the state was expected to provide for all needs. This dependency culture was found not only behind the Iron Curtain, but also in all our societies. The culture of "the professional knows best"—be it in medicine, psychology, psychoanalysis, or whatever field—was part of this condition. In Europe, many of the large, socially inspired government systems were put in place following the depredations of the second World War. The British National Health Service founded in 1948 was one of them, and at one stage was the world's third largest employer after the Soviet army and the Indian railways.

Such mega-dependency systems followed the fight-flight basic assumption of the Second World War and could only come into existence because there was a general wish for a system on which all could depend. Today, dependency is out of fashion. All organizations that were the providers of this social need and their office bearers are now up for questioning. For example, in the United Kingdom, university teachers, other educators, lawyers, architects, and doctors have all had their working practices examined, and some have had their professional systems dismantled. This attack on professionalism is evident in the recent change in the United Kingdom, where "architect"—once a protected designation for a profession—is now a term that anyone can use. Nor have politicians been immune from attack, and their public image stands at a particular low. They, in turn, have been eager to pass the blame on to others. Dissatisfaction with them often moves down a lightning rod of their own making, ending in various governmental committees investigating the failings of others.

The breakdown of the previous global system and general disillusionment with a dependency model are, I believe, the two key factors in the changed climate. A worldwide recession adds to our difficulties.

A final factor is communication, which has become much more devious. Everyone is now aware of underlying anxieties, and communiqués are now written so as to avoid stirring them up. The price of doing so—lost votes, poor poll ratings, a drop in the stock market—can make the difference between success and bankruptcy. A language that we are familiar with from the euphemisms of the Vietnam war has been polished and refined so that, for example, a report that spells the death knell for many services in the heartland of the United Kingdom is called "Making London Better."

CHANGES IN THE MENTAL HEALTH FIELD

I have so far concentrated on some of the factors that have made for change in the wider frame. There are also changes in the mental health field. Over the past twenty years there has been a revolution in how we treat seriously ill patients, particularly when it comes to decisions about hospitalization. Some of this work was done in the United States, much of it in Italy and Scandinavia. Many institutions have closed and thousands of patients are now treated in the community. Many of us believe that the process has gone too far and is no longer determined by patient or clinical need, but is instead driven by doctrinaire processes.

These changes have affected the identity of psychiatrists. For many, being in charge of an inpatient unit was a key component of psychiatric work, including diagnostic sessions, prescribing medication, reviewing patients, and leading teams. With the closure of institutions, that role has been abolished. The result in the United Kingdom and elsewhere in Europe has been a crisis of professional identity.

Psychiatrists have increasingly moved from institutions into individual treatment, previously the domain of psychoanalysts and psychotherapists. Many of these "professional migrants" have not undertaken the additional training required by this shift. Instead, they have adopted quick-fix psychotherapeutic techniques, or added medication to the psychotherapeutic process.

I am not suggesting that short-term therapies are inappropriate, nor am I saying that medication should not be used as an adjunct to psychotherapy in certain circumstances. I am referring to an unfortunate development in which displaced professionals move into other areas of work without having had adequate training or re-training. As part of the social process of establishing themselves, many have developed a stance of attacking existing practitioners in the field, decrying their methods, and questioning their success rate and their fees. In addition to this group, a great many poorly trained practitioners released from very dubious training organizations that make enormous and unsubstantiated claims on behalf of their techniques have invaded the practice of psychiatry.

We thus find ourselves, both as clinicians and as organizations, harassed from all sides, and in general we have been slow to respond. In the United Kingdom we went through a phase of attempting to ignore these changes and hoping that they would go away. That was coupled with a belief that our "innate excellence" would see off the intruders. It proved not to be so.

Next there was an exodus of sorts from institutions with senior professionals withdrawing into full-time private practice, sometimes accompanied by implications that institutional life was no longer a suitable place for those with serious intention to make their mark in psychoanalysis or psychoanalytic psychotherapy. In doing so, they undermined not only their institutions, but also the general morale of those who valued psychoanalysis.

Similar changes have occurred in psychoanalytic institutes, as a form of institutional acting out arising from a set of unconscious institutional anxieties. The institutes feel themselves threatened and at risk of going under. In response, they fall into a defensive mode which focuses on a them-and-us state of mind—the institutional equivalent of a paranoid/schizoid process as described by Melanie Klein (1946). By this means, clarity or, more accurately, pseudo-clarity appears, and psychoanalysts feel certain about who is on one side and who is on the other. Battle lines are drawn. Institutes revert to teaching the pure gold of psychoanalysis. Anything else, including applications of psychoanalytic principles, is seen as a dilution. In Menzies' (1960) terms, the institution has structured itself, its functioning, and how it presents itself through a set of defences against primitive anxieties, instead of task-oriented arrangements. Such arrangements are counterproductive because they alienate the very groups needed to provide a beachhead into application of psychoanalytic ideas in the community and open the risk of the institute being accused of elitism.

THE PRESENT SITUATION

The situation is gloomy. In the past few years, however, there has been a turning point in our capacity to present our views and underline the worth of our professional practices and insights. I believe that it is possible to retain the essential psychoanalytic core of the psychoanalytic organization, while at the same time working actively at application to everyday life in a much wider professional and lay mental health field.

The Tavistock Clinic is a large (200 staff members, 1,200 students) multi-layered, complex organization. Many of the senior training staff are psychoanalysts; intensive psychoanalytic work is the foundation of several key courses, while at the same time application of psychoanalytic ideas goes on at several levels of intensity.

In organizations with a different structure, the application component could be a clearly demarcated discrete sector of the organization with a different task, or, alternatively, the application element could be done by cooperation with a separate independent organization that is suited to perform an applied role.

We have begun to initiate significant changes at the Tavistock Clinic in response to the factors I have outlined in this chapter.

- a shift from a purely academic pursuit of knowledge to a more applied approach
- a shift from a general research approach to a study of costs and outcome
- a shift from a consulting approach to a more managerial one
- a shift in emphasis from a provider approach to services to a consumer-led approach.

These are major changes in how we conduct ourselves in the clinical, academic, research, and managerial fields. In many instances these required changes could prove to be to our advantage.

THE SHIFT FROM ACADEMICS TO APPLICATION

The shift to a more applied approach in our academic pursuits opens possibilities for change in a much wider field. Isobel Menzies-Lyth, in her classic paper "A Case Study in the Functioning of Social Systems as a Defense Against Anxiety" (1960), suggests that organizational structures are often determined by a process of escaping the pain, anxieties, and difficulties arising from psychoanalytic work. I believe that some of our academic pursuits have increasingly been derailed by similar anxieties—after all, we are expected to tackle some of the most difficult and resistant problems in human behavior and society. In England, it is essential to have a substantial list of academic publications in order to get a job as a consultant in the National Health Service. Many of the papers written are more determined by a need to have a long list of publications than by any true academic or research interests. Academic pursuits allow us an escape from daily work tensions, while at the same time drawing us into technical arguments among ourselves that often serve almost wholly defensive needs. We mock the medieval church debates about how many angels could be accommodated on the head of a pin, but many of the arguments in the field of psychotherapy or psychoanalysis have a similar irrational intensity. A move toward greater application and therefore greater openness to review by others can be of substantial help in overcoming our isolation and integrating our ideas with the rest of society.

THE SHIFT FROM RESEARCH TO OUTCOME

In the research area, there is a greater awareness of the need to show the outcome and cost benefits arising from our work. While none of us would have any doubts about defending research for the sake of pure research, much research that is undertaken nowadays is what one might call "pseudo research," where the epistemophylic instinct is absent, and other factors, such as the gain of personal status, are the benefit. The pressure nowadays is therefore to show that the research and work activities we undertake produce relevant results and benefit society. Paradoxically, this approach can also help us. If preliminary evidence suggests that intervention arising from a research pilot project might have a major cost-benefit advantage, it is then very difficult for the potential funders of that research to turn down the project. We are all increasingly aware that we have been too modest in our claims of the cost-benefit advantages of psychotherapeutic intervention in the cycle of psychosocial illness, particularly if we take into account the enormous cost in lost working hours, taxes, and the use of medical services. In this field the work of many Scandinavian psychoanalysts and psychiatrists has been of great help, as has work done in Germany. In the United Kingdom, the Association for Psychoanalytic Psychotherapy in the National Health Service (APP) has organized these data and publications. Much more work needs to be done, but I believe the tide to be changing in our favor.

THE SHIFT FROM CONSULTATION TO MANAGEMENT

The shift from a consultation approach to a more managerial one is widespread. In the United Kingdom, the model of a democratic partnership between doctors to deliver services as agreed with administrators was popular in the late 1970s and early 1980s. It failed because it delivered neither the promise nor the service, but instead caused a great deal of irritation and delay on both sides. The reason for this was that not enough attention was paid to the primary task of the arrangement, nor was there sufficient awareness of the destructive, anti-task group processes that slowed down and at times entirely sabotaged the decision-making process.

But all is not lost. It is possible for doctors to take on some, or at times all, of the managerial functions with a substantial democratic consultative component, while retaining the benefit of having final authority. The key here is whether we as professionals are also prepared to become budget managers; the purse strings, of course, confirm ultimate power.

THE SHIFT FROM PROVIDER TO CONSUMER

The shift from a provider-led system of care to a consumer-led one was in the long run inevitable. Provider-led services can only function if there is a central bureaucracy and an agreed upon state of dependency on it, in which consumers do not question what the bureaucracy delivers—be it Russian shoes, East German cars, or certain models of psychiatry.

With the shift away from dependency, there is now a greater need for the mental health system to listen to what the consumer wants and to deliver what the consumer needs. This applies to psychoanalysis as much as to any other field in mental health. One of the flaws of this approach is, of course, that the consumer often knows neither what he or she needs nor what a realistic expectation of the service might be. But the fact that there is a problem with conveying information does not mean that the operation should not be attempted. The greater media attention that all health services, and mental health services in particular, are enjoying offers opportunities for increased consumer sophistication. If the public are better informed, there is an increased chance of their demanding our services, and conveying this demand to the funding authorities.

SOME THOUGHTS ABOUT OUR FUTURE

As members of organizations that go about our therapeutic work along psychoanalytic lines, often on a residential basis, we are laboring under the disadvantages outlined earlier in this chapter. We may, however, lose sight of the fact that we also have some clear advantages. These are perhaps best captured in the title of this book, *The Inner World in the Outer World*. What we have that is precious, if not unique, is integration. The fact is that we not only focus on the inner world and its vicissitudes, but do so in the context of the interaction with the outer world. This opportunity to focus on both—the inner world in therapy or analysis and the outer world in family or group or community structures—makes for a powerful combination that few therapeutic settings can offer the individual patient in his or her quest for improvement.

We also have available the application of psychoanalytic understanding to group and institutional processes along the lines pioneered by A. K. Rice and others, first at the Tavistock and later through the A. K. Rice Institute in the United States. This not only harnesses powerful therapeutic processes, but also, equally importantly, contributes substantially to reducing the acting out of psychopathology of patients and staff alike.

Our organizations are well placed to provide the training needs of a variety of mental health professionals who aspire to work in an integrated and integrative way. This provides a multi-disciplinary and cooperative approach that has the best chance of standing up against the siren voices of the sectarian groupings—be they professionally or theoretically based.

It may seem odd to introduce the concept of envy at the end of this book, but I believe that one of the reactions we elicit in others is envy, particularly of our integrative communal team approach. Envy from others—and the resultant attack and spoiling—may contribute to the increasing isolation and lack of support from all sides that many independent psychoanalysts and other mental health workers experience. The path to resolving this envy is openness—in our relationships with colleagues and referrers, and in the expansion of our consultancy and assessment services. In doing so, our perceived elitism is reduced, and we are seen as both helpful and at times just as stumped by problems as anyone else. Collaborative research ventures are also well worth embarking on, helping to break down the them-and-us interinstitutional rivalries.

Finally, and perhaps most important, we need to be part of the public debate about the mental health of our nations and of the world. For too long we have hidden in our consulting rooms or institutions, or in our specialist journals in which we have addressed no one but ourselves. There have been massive changes in our attitude. I hope this book will add to the impetus of our being firmly part of the debate. It is up to us not only to know the cost of what we are producing, but to make absolutely sure that the value is publicly recognized.

REFERENCES

Bion, W. R. (1961). *Experiences in Groups.* London: Tavistock.

Dicks, H. V. (1967). *Marital Tensions.* New York: Basic Books.

———. (1972). *License and Mass Murder.* New York: Basic Books.

Freud, S. (1913). *Totem and Taboo. Standard Edition.* 13:1–161.

———. (1930). *Civilization and Its Discontents. Standard Edition.* 21:64–145.

———. (1939). *Moses and Monotheism. Standard Edition.* 23:7–137.

Klein, M. (1946). Notes on some schizoid mechanisms. *International Journal of Psycho-analysis,* 27:99–110.

Lawrence, W. G. (1979). *Exploring Individual and Organizational Boundaries.* Chichester, England, and New York: Wiley.

Menzies, I. E. P. (1960). A case study in the functioning of social systems as a defense against anxiety. *Human Relations,* 13:95–121.

Miller, E. (1993). *From Dependency to Autonomy.* London: Free Association Books.

Money-Kyrle, R. E. (1961). *Man's Picture of His World.* New York: International Universities Press.

Rice, A. K. (1970). *Productivity and Social Organization.* London and New York: Tavistock.

Shapiro, E. R., and A. W. Carr. (1991). *Lost in Familiar Places: Creating New Connections between the Individual and Society.* New Haven and London: Yale University Press.

Turquet, P. M. (1975). Threats to identity in the large group. In *The Large Group: Dynamics and Therapy,* L. Kreeger, ed. London: Constable.

Index

Abelin, E. L., 17
Aeschylus: *Oresteia*, 150
Agamemnon, 5, 147–51
Aggression: bureaucratization and, 4, 106, 110, 115, 116; in groups, 4, 97–99, 100, 104, 110, 113, 116–17
Analyst, 39, 40, 47, 54; neutrality of, 28, 39, 40; role of, 2, 38, 47, 48–49, 52–53, 54
Anzieu, D., 99
Art. *See* Creativity

Austen Riggs Center, ix; management structure, 18–19
Authoritarian personality, 104, 115

Bakhtin, M., 47, 53–54
Balint, M., 49
Bion, W. R., 17, 83, 97, 99, 127, 171, 173
Bipersonal field, 2
Bisexuality: creativity and, 91–92; Freud on, 86

183

Blue Cross/Blue Shield utilization
review, 15
Bonaparte, M., 62, 64
Boundaries, 4; the enemy and, 5,
127–28, 130, 133, 135, 138, 139;
outer world, 10, 74
Breuer, J., 152–53, 156
Brickman, H. R., 17
Brown, Lyn Mikel, 158
Bureaucratization, 4, 5, 99,
105–09, 115, 116, 117–19; aggression and, 4, 106, 110, 115,
116; characteristics of, 105;
democracy and, 118; ideology
and, 108, 109–10; legal, 109,
117; medical, 108; sadism in,
106, 107, 108, 113, 117; as self-
serving, 105, 107, 108

Canetti, E., 99
Carr, Wesley, 171
Changes, 1, 7, 12; in certainty,
171–72; economic pressures, 7,
14, 15, 16; in focus, 5, 6, 172;
time frame, 9, 13, 14, 15. See also
Managed care; Mental health
care
Chasseguet-Smirgel, J., 99
Child abuse: bureaucracy and, 109
Child development, 5, 50–51, 171;
boys vs. girls, 5, 163–65
Clarity, 171, 172, 176
Cognitive revolution, 74
Communication, 53, 174
Community vs. society, 119
Complementary attitude, 54
Conformity, 3, 27, 28–31, 34, 35,
38, 40; inclusion of, 36–37; sur-

prises and, 31; treatment for, 30,
32, 36
Contradiction, 160
Costs: shifting of, 15, 16
Countertransference, 12, 40, 38,
49; characterological, 39; Freud
and, 44–45
Creativity, 4, 77; anal aspects of,
85–86, 89, 90; artist's medium,
4, 82–83; blockages to, 83, 84,
86–87, 92–93, 95; Freud on,
77–78; inner world and, 8, 81,
84–85; mother-child and, 51, 78;
outer world and, 81; play and,
78; productivity and, 79; public
and, 4, 80–81, 83, 86, 94, 95;
sexual aspects of, 81, 84–85, 86,
87, 89, 91–92, 95; spontaneous
gesture, 51; stability and, 79; violence and, 78–79, 84–85, 95

Decision-making: aggression and,
99; functional vs. democratic,
103, 111–12; patient involvement, 19
DeKoninck, J., 63
Democracy, 110, 111, 151; bureaucracy and, 105, 118; decision-
making in, 103, 111–12
Democratization of personhood,
34, 36
Dependency, 5, 15, 97, 99, 173–74,
180
Deutsch, Helene, 54
Dicks, Henry, 171
Disengagement, 51
Dissociation, 145, 160; Freud on,
165; patriarchy and, 5, 161,

164–66; talking cure and, 154,
156, 157; trauma and, 54
Dreams, 59; apt personal representation, 71; assimilation, 69–70,
72; Freud on, 60, 62, 65; higher-
order aim, 71, 73; homomorphic, 60, 65–68, 74; isomorphic,
61–65; Lion Hunter, 64, 65, 68,
73; metonymy, 68–69; phases,
61; transformations, 68–69, 70,
71–73; traumatic, 59–65, 68, 74
Durkheim, E., 119

Egalitarian ideology, 110, 117,
118, 119
Ego, 45–46, 47, 98, 127
Eliot, George, 164
Empathy, 51–52, 54
Enemy, 5, 123; appeasement,
131–32; assimilation of, 131–32;
boundaries, 5, 127–28, 130, 133,
135, 138, 139; definition, 125;
dialogue with, 5, 125, 126, 130,
135–36, 138, 139, 140; divisiveness, 128; external, 98, 129; intrapsychic level, 126–27; moratorium, 128; neighbors as,
139–40; oedipal, 5, 126–27,
136–38, 139, 140; otherness, 5,
125, 127, 132–33, 137, 140;
peace, 128, 129, 132; preoedipal,
5, 126, 136, 138, 139, 140;
strangeness, 132–33, 137; symbols, 5, 136–37
England: National Health Service,
174, 178; professionalism in, 174
Enmity, 5, 124, 128–29, 134; definition, 125

Envy, 3, 109, 111, 181
Erikson, Erik, 2, 32, 34, 161, 162
Euripides, 147, 165; *Iphigenia in
Aulis*, 150
Externalization, 9, 16, 140; artists
and, 80
External managerial frame, 81

Fairbairn, W. D., 44, 46, 47, 54
False self, 34, 49
Family (of patient), 18
Father, role of, 2, 17; in hysteria,
153, 154–55, 157
Ferenczi, S., 45, 52, 54
Financial managers, 16, 17
Fisher, C., 62
Fliess, Wilhelm, 45, 153, 154
Flight-fight, 97, 99, 174
Focus, change in, 6; global vs. lo-
cal, 5, 172, 174
Fragmentation of self, 33, 82
Framework, therapeutic, 3, 10–12;
third parties in, 18
Frank, Anne, 160–61, 162
French revolution, 119
Freud, S., 39, 44, 113, 163, 170,
171; on bisexuality, 86; on creativity, 77–78; on discomfort of
culture, 151; on dissociation of
self, 165; dreams and, 60, 62, 65;
on ego, 45–46, 47; on hysteria,
152, 153–56, 157; on idealization of leader, 97, 98; on incest,
153, 154; mass psychology, 104,
116, 134; on memory, 47; on patient's family, 18; on psychology
of the individual, 44, 46; on self-
destructiveness, 80; stimuli,

Freud, S. (*continued*)
62–63, 65; on voice, 153; on war,
124, 130, 134

Gabbard, Glen, 15, 16
Gays, pressure on, 40
Gender stereotypes, 40
Gilligan, C., 158
Global vs. local focus, 5, 172, 174
Group(s), 173; aggression in, 4,
97–99, 100, 104, 110, 113,
116–17; authority, 103, 104,
112; basic assumption vs.
work, 173; defensive aspects of, 97, 98,
100, 104, 105, 115, 116; dynamics, 98, 135, 173; enmity within,
128–29; ideology, 4, 5, 99, 100,
108, 109–15, 116, 117–18; individual and, 173; leadership, 4,
98–99, 100–02, 104, 106, 111,
112–13, 116, 130; loss of identity in, 97, 98; narcissism and, 4,
98, 99, 104, 107–08, 111, 113,
116; paranoia of, 4, 5, 100–05,
106, 107, 110, 111, 112, 115,
116; politics, 102–03; regression
in, 97, 99, 100, 101, 102, 104,
105, 106, 116; small, 99, 135,
138; totalitarian, 4, 113, 114,
117, 118. *See also* Bureaucratization

Hartmann, H., 46
Hegel, G. W. F., 48
Homosexuality, 40, 91
Hospitalization, 14, 175
Hospitals: bureaucracy, 108
Hysteria, 152–56, 157, 166

Identity: conformity and, 28; diffusion, 34; female, 5, 163–65;
groups and, 97, 129; loss of, 97,
98; male, 5, 164–65; negative,
32; at risk, 3, 34
Ideology: bureaucratization and,
108, 109–10; groups and, 4, 5,
99, 108, 109–15, 116, 117–18
Incest, 153, 154–55, 157
Individual: focus on, 43; Freud on,
44, 46; in group, 173; rights, 97,
98, 110
Individualism, 3, 27, 32–34, 38, 40,
129; treatment, 33, 36–37
Infant. *See* Mother-child interactions
Inner world-outer world, 2, 3;
boys, 5, 164; girls, 5, 163–65
Insurance companies, 10, 21–22
Interpretation, 7–10, 12, 16; man-
aged care and, 13, 14, 15–16, 18
Intersubjectivity, 2, 11, 17, 43, 44,
48, 50
Intervention, 13–14, 22
Introjective identification, 131
Iphigenia, 5, 147–50, 161, 165
Israel, 124, 125, 138, 139

Jacobson, E., 46
Jacques, Elliot, 100, 105
Joseph, Betty, 30

Kernberg, O., 46, 47
Klein, Melanie, 29, 78, 130, 161,
171, 176
Kohut, Heinz, 48
Kolakowski, L., 114, 119
Koulack, D., 63

Lacan, J., 2, 17
Language acquisition, 50, 51
Lawrence, Gordon, 171
Leadership, 4, 101–02, 106; as boundary function, 130; idealized, 97, 98, 99, 104, 106; mediocrity in, 4, 99, 104, 111; paranoid, 112, 116
Legal bureaucracy, 109, 117
Les Atrides (Mnouchkine), 150–51
Lewis, H., 62
Liberty, 119
Linklater, Kristin, 157
Loewenstein, R., 66, 68, 69
Luther, Martin, 162–63

Male identity, 5, 164–65
Malia, M., 114
Managed care, 2, 23; authority of, 10, 18, 23; costs of, 15, 16; interpretation and, 13, 14, 15–16, 18; negotiated, 19–20; time limits, 9, 13, 14, 15. See also Mental health care
Management, 7; analyst's, 11–12; interpretation and, 12, 16
Marxist theory, 114, 115, 118
Masters, R. D., 102, 105, 106
Maury, L. F. A., 62, 65
Meanings, new, 52–53, 55
Memory, 47, 54
Mental health care, 1, 2, 12, 175–78; consultation vs. management, 6, 177, 179; costs, 15, 16; hospitalization, 14, 175; professional exodus, 176; provider- vs. consumer-led, 6, 177, 180; research vs. applied, 6,

177, 178–79; symptom management, 1, 14; time frame, 9, 13, 14, 15
Menuchin, Salvador, 109
Menzies, I. E. P., 176, 178
Michels, R., 118
Miller, Eric, 171
Miller, Jean Baker, 159
Milner, M., 10
Mnouchkine, Ariane, 150–51
Modell, A. H., 80, 83
Money-Kyrle, Roger, 171
Mother-child interactions, 50–51, 132, 136; art and, 78
Muller, J., 23
Multiple self-narratives, 36

Nachträglichkeit, 47
Narcissism, 33, 49, 50; creativity and, 91, 95; groups and, 4, 98, 99, 104, 107–08, 111, 113, 116; of minor difference, 133, 140
Negotiated terms, 10, 19–20
Nesbit, R., 119
Noel, Normi, 157–58

Object relations, 44, 47, 97, 99, 133, 161
Object representations, 46, 98
Oedipal interactions, 104, 137–38, 154, 163
Ogden, T. H., 2, 11, 17
Omnipotence, illusions of, 33
Orestes, 150–51, 164
Organizations: requisite and paranoiagenic, 100–02; structure, 178. See also Group(s)
Outer-world boundaries, 10, 74

Patriarchy, 151, 153, 162; dissociation and, 5, 158, 161, 164–66; internalization of, 156, 164
Paul, I., 62
Personality disorders, 7; as adaptive, 8; family and, 8, 18; nature of, 9; repetition in, 22; treatment, 14, 16, 21–22
Pessoa, Fernando, 77
Piaget, J., 69
Plakun, Eric, 19
Plaut, A., 10
Politics, institutional, 102
Pregenital erotism, 4, 84–85, 87, 92, 95
Premature foreclosure, 34
Professionalism, attack on, 174
Professionals, exodus of, 176
Projective identification, 53–55, 131, 171, 172, 173
Psychiatry, changes in, 1, 2, 9, 175–76, 178–80
Psychoanalysis, 2, 43
Psychoanalysts for the Prevention of Nuclear War, 124
Psychopathology, 160
Public: artist and, 4, 80–81, 83, 86, 94, 95

Racker, H., 54
Rappaport, E., 65, 66
Reality, 37, 55
Regulation of distance, 49
Reich, Annie, 39
Relational theory, 44, 49
Relationships, 159; Freud on, 44; men, 164–65; voice and, 5, 160,

164; women and, 15, 163, 164, 165, 166
Renik, O., 62
Research: cost-benefit, 179; vs. applied, 6, 177, 178–79
Resource management, 8, 13, 15–16, 21
Rice, Ken, 171, 181
Rickman, John, 44

Sadism, bureaucratic, 106, 107, 108, 113, 117
Sander, Lou, 51
Schafer, R., 81–82, 86
Segal, Hanna, 86
Self: autonomous vs. dependent, 48, 50; Doing vs. Being, 128, 132; false, 34, 49; fragmentation of, 33, 82; Freud and, 45, 46, 47; language and, 50, 51; as paradoxical, 3, 47, 48, 50, 51, 55, 83; private vs. social, 3–4, 47–51
Selfhood, democratization of, 34, 36
Self representations, 46, 98
Sexual abuse: children, 52, 154; hysteria and, 153
Sexuality, creativity and, 81, 84–85, 86, 87, 89, 91–92, 95; pregenital, 4, 84–85, 87, 92, 95
Shapiro, Edward R., 3, 80–81, 171
Siegel, A., 68
Silk, K., 14
Sinyavsky, A., 114
Soviet Union, 107, 108, 110, 114, 118, 119, 173
Speech. See Voice

Sperry, R., 74
Splitting mechanisms, 171, 172
Steiner, John, 31
Stern, D. N., 127
Strachey, J., 45
Strengthening Healthy Resistance
  and Courage in Girls project,
  157
Structural theory, 44
Suggestion, 52
Superego, 44, 45, 104, 115
Sutherland, J., 46
Symptom management, 1, 14

Talking cure, 153–54, 156, 157,
  166
Tavistock Clinic, 177
Tavistock Group Relations Con-
  ferences, 127
Tavistock Institute of Human Re-
  lations, 171
Terr, L., 62, 67
Therapeutic framework, 10–12,
  17, 22; changes, 9, 23
Therapist. See Analyst
Therapy: as dialogue, 40
"Third," the: for artists, 80; ene-
  mies and, 5; in oedipal develop-
  ment, 136–38; in therapy, 7–8,
  16, 17–18, 21
Thought transfer, 54
Time limits (for treatment), 9, 13,
  14, 15
Tocqueville, A. de, 118

Tönnies, F., 119
Transference, 12, 18, 19, 21, 31,
  43; countertransference, 12, 38,
  39, 40, 44–45, 49; Freud and, 44,
  47; nature of, 48–49, 55; negative, 15, 39; relationships, 35,
  37–38, 39
Transgression, 81, 95
Trevarthen, C., 50
Turquet, Pierre, 97, 99, 173

Van der Kolk, B., 62
Ventriloquation, 53
Voice, 160, 163, 164; change in,
  146, 147, 166; loss of, 5, 153; relationships and, 5, 160, 164; resonance and, 157, 166
Volkan, V. D., 124, 126, 133, 139,
  140
Voslensky, M., 114

Weber, M., 118
Wharton, Edith, 146, 161
Winnicott, D. W., 4, 49, 51, 78,
  128, 136
Witkin, H., 62, 68
Women: development, 5, 160,
  163–66; hysteria, 152–54, 166;
  relationships, 15, 163, 164, 165,
  166; shame, 149. See also Patriarchy; Voice
Woolf, Virginia, 145–46

Zinoviev, A., 110